INDEX.

SPRING.

No. 1.

OVERTURE,

Expressing the passage from WINTER *to* SPRING.

fz
fz
fz
fz
fz
fz
fz
fz
fz
fz
A
p
3
3
3

f
B
f
fz
fz
fz
fz
fz
fz
fz
fz
fz
fz
fz

fz
fz
fz
fz
fz
fz
fz
fz
fz
fz
fz
fz
C
f
f
p
f
f
fz
fz
fz

fz
fz
dim.
p
ff
fz
fz
p
f
D
ff
ff
fz
fz
fz
fz
fz
fz
fz
fz
sempre f

No. 2. RECIT.—"BEHOLD WHERE SURLY WINTER FLIES."

SIMON.

Be- hold where sur-ly Win-ter flies!

f

Far to the north he passes off.

f

He calls his ruf - fian blasts,

f

His ruf-fian blasts o-bey, and

quit the howl-ing hill.

f *p* *fz* *p* *fz* *p* *fz* *p* *fz* *p* *ff*

LUCAS.

Be-hold, from craggy rocks the snows

In livid torrents melted run!

Adagio. 𝅗𝅥 = 69.
dol.
Adagio.
dol.
f
JANE.
Forth fly the te - pid
ten.
airs, And from the southern shores al - lure
The
p
dol.
mes - sen - ger of Spring.
dol.

No. 3. Chorus.—"COME, GENTLE SPRING."

A
Come, . come, gen-tle Spring! . . bid drowsy na-ture rise, bid
Come, . come, gen-tle Spring! . . bid drowsy na-ture rise, bid
Come, gen-tle Spring! bid drow sy na-ture rise, bid
Come, . come, gen-tle Spring! . . bid drow-sy na-ture rise, bid
drow-sy na-ture rise,
drow-sy na-ture rise, bid drowsy na-ture rise, . . bid drowsy na-ture
drow-sy na-ture rise, bid drow-sy na-ture rise, . . bid drow-sy na-ture
drow-sy na-ture rise, bid drow-sy na-ture rise, . . bid drow-sy na-ture
. . O come, gen-tle Spring! e-the-real mildness, come!
rise, O come, gen-tle, gen-tle Spring! e-the-real mildness, come!
rise, O come, gen-tle, gen-tle Spring! e-the-real mild-ness, come!
rise, O come, come, gen-tle Spring! e-the-real mildness, come!
dol.

B

Come, gentle Spring! ethereal mildness, come. Come, gentle

Come, gentle Spring! e-the-real mildness, come. Come, gentle

Come, gentle Spring! O come, Come, gentle

Come, gentle Spring,

Spring, come, gentle Spring, e-the-real, e-

Spring, come, gentle Spring, e-the-real, e-

Spring, come, gentle Spring, e-the-real, e-

come, gentle Spring, gentle Spring, e-the-real, e-

-the-real mildness, come.

-the-real mildness, come.

-the-real mildness, come.

-the-real mildness, come.

GIRLS AND WOMEN.

C

Soprano 1mo. See, gentle Spring de-

Soprano 2do. See, gentle Spring de-

Alto 1mo. See, gentle Spring de-

Alto 2do. See, gentle Spring de-

-light - ful comes! Her soft and balm - y
breath we feel, The joy of re - no - vat - ed life.
See, gen - tle Spring, see, gen - tle Spring de - light - ful

comes! . . see, gen - tle Spring de - light - - ful comes!
comes! see, gen - tle Spring de - light - - ful comes!
comes! . . see, gen - tle Spring de - light - - ful comes!
comes! . . see, gen - tle Spring de - light - ful comes!
cres.
D
MEN.—Tenor 1mo. (8ve lower).
As yet the year is un - confirm'd, as yet the year is
Tenor 2do (8ve. lower).
As yet the year is un confirm'd, as yet the year is
Bass 1mo.
As yet the year is un - confirm'd, as yet the year is
Bass 2do.
As yet the year is un - confirm'd, as yet the year is
D
un - confirm'd, And oft, . . and oft re - turn-ing Win - ter's blast, or
un - confirm'd, And oft, . . and oft re - turn-ing Win - ter's blast, or
un - confirm'd, And oft, . . and oft re - turn-ing Win - ter's blast, or
un - confirm'd, And oft, . . and oft re - turn-ing Win - ter's blast, or

black en - ve - nom'd fog, . . . the bud and bloom des - troys, the
black en - ve - nom'd fog, . . . the bud and bloom des - troys, the
black en - ve - nom'd fog, . . . the bud and bloom des - troys, the
black en - ve - nom'd fog, . . . the bud and bloom des - troys, the
fz
fz
fz
p
bud . . and bloom destroys.
bud . . and bloom destroys.
bud . . and bloom destroys.
bud . . and bloom destroys.
ff
p
Treble.
E
p
Come, gen - tle Spring, . . e - the - real mild - ness,
Alto.
p
Come, gen - tle Spring, . . e - the - real mild - ness,
Tenor
(8ve. lower.)
p
Come, gen - tle Spring, . . e - the - real mild - ness,
Bass.
p
f
Come, gen - tle Spring, . . e -
E
pp

come! . . come, come, And smil - ing on our
come! - . come, come, And smil - ing on our
come! . - e - the - real mild - ness, come! And smil - ing on our
- the - real mildness, come! And smil - ing on our plains descend,
legato.
plains descend; O come, gen-tle Spring, O come, while mu - sic wakes a -
plains descend; O come, gen-tle Spring, O come, while mu - sic wakes a
plains descend; O come, gen-tle Spring, while mu - sic wakes a -
come, gen - tle Spring, O come, gen - tle Spring, while mu - sic wakes a -
F
- round, . . O come, O come, while mu-sic wakes a - round, . . while
- round, O come, O come, O come, while mu-sic wakes a - round, . . while
- round, O come, O come, while mu - sic wakes a - round, - . while
- round, O come, O come, O come, while mu-sic wakes a - round, . . while
F

mu - sic wakes a - round. O come, and smil - - ing

mu - sic wakes a - round. O come, and smil - - ing

mu - sic wakes a - round. O come, and smil - - ing

mu - sic wakes a - round. O come, and smil - - ing

on our plains de - scend, . . and smil - - - ing on our plains de -

on our plains de - scend, descend, and smil - - - ing on our plains de -

on our plains de - scend, descend, and smil - - - ing on our plains de -

on our plains de - scend, . . and on . . . . our plains . . de -

- scend, O come, come, come!

- scend, O come, come, come!

- scend, O come, come, come!

- scend, O come, come, come

No. 4.
RECIT.—"AT LAST THE BOUNTEOUS SUN."
SIMON.
VOICE.
At last the bounteous sun From Aries into Taurus rolls, Wide spreading life and heat; The fleecy
ACCOMP.
f
clouds up - rise sublime, And stretch their thin and sil-ver wings O'er all-sur-round-ing heaven.
f
No. 5.
AIR.—"WITH JOY THE IMPATIENT HUSBANDMAN."
Allegretto. ♩ = 88.
VOICE.
ACCOMP.
f
SIMON.
With joy th'im-pa-tient hus - band-man Drives
p
forth his lus-ty team To where the well-us'd plough remains, Now loosen'd from the

frost,
With
ten.
ten.
f
joy th'im - pa - tient hus-bandman Drives forth his lus-ty team
ten.
p
pp
ten.
To where the well-us'd plough remains, Now loosen'd from the frost; To
where the well- us'd plough remains, Now loosen'd from the frost;
To where the well- us'd plough remains, Now loos-en'd from the frost; To

where the well-us'd plough remains, Now loosen'd from the frost, ... Now
loosen'd from the frost, from the frost.
8ves.
With measur'd step he throws the grain, with measur'd step he throws the grain with-
- in the bounteous earth. O sun, soft
show'rs and dews! O sun, soft show'rs and dews! The gold - - en
ten.

ears in plen - ty bring; The gold - - -
sempre p
ten.
- - - - - - - - - - - - - - - - -
8ves.
- - - - en ears in plen - - - - - ty, in plen - ty
bring! With mea-sur'd step he throws the grain, With
f
p
measur'd step he throws the grain within the bounteous earth.
f

O sun, soft show'rs and dews! The gold - en ears in plen - ty, in
cres.
p
plen - ty bring!
f
fz
fz
fz
With joy th'impatient husbandman Drives forth his lus-ty team To
p.
where the well-us'd plough remains, Now loosen'd from the frost;
ten.
And they their wonted toil be-gin, Made cheer-ful by a song And

they their wont-ed toil be-gin, Made cheer-ful by a song,
And they their wont-ed toil be-gin, Made cheer-ful by a song, and
they their wont-ed toil be-gin, Made cheer-ful by a song, . . . made
cheer-ful by a song, by a song. . . . by a
song, by a song. . . . .
pp
p
pp
p
pp

No. 6. Recit.—"LABORIOUS MAN HATH DONE HIS PART."
LUCAS.
Tenor.
Accomp.
Laborious man hath done his part; And while his heart with hope expands, That
na-ture's friend-ly aid Will rich-ly crown his toil, His ar-dent prayers,
his ar - - dent prayers to heaven as-cend.
f
No. 7. Trio and Chorus.—"BE PROPITIOUS, BOUNTEOUS HEAVEN."
Poco Adagio.
Solo.—LUCAS.
Voice.
Accomp.
♩=72.
dolce.
p
Be pro-pi-tious, boun-teous heaven, O'er the hills,
o'er the hills and vales lux-u-riant Spread a rich autumnal feast!
8ves.
cres.

A
Tutti.
Be pro - pi - tious, boun - - teous hea - ven,
O'er the hills, o'er the hills and vales lux-u - - riant
spread a rich au-tum-nal feast!
ten.
cres.
fz
p
mezzo

Haydn's "Seasons' (Spring).—Novello, Ewer and Co's Octavo Edition.

crown'd, . . . And songs of joy thy praise shall
crown'd, . . . And songs of joy thy praise shall
crown'd, . . . And songs of joy thy praise shall
pp
B
Solo.
tell. Be pro-pi - tious, bounteous
Solo.
tell. Be pro-pi - tious, bounteous
Solo.
tell. Be pro-pi - tious, bounteous
Treble.
Tutti.
Be pro - pi - tious, boun - teous
Alto.
Tutti.
Be pro - pi - tious, boun - teous
Tenor (8ve. lower.)
Tutti.
Be pro - pi - tious, boun - teous
Bass.
Tutti.
Be pro - pi - tious, boun - teous
B
cres.
f

hea - ven!
hea - ven!
hea - ven!
hea - ven! O'er the hills, o'er the hills and vales lux -
hea - ven! O'er the hills, o'er the hills and vales lux -
hea - ven! O'er the hills, o'er the hills and vales lux -
hea - ven! O'er the hills, o'er the hills and vales lux -
- u - - riant spread a rich au-tum-nal feast!
- u - - riant spread a rich au-tum-nal feast!
u - - riant spread a rich au-tum-nal feast!
- u - - riant spread a rich au-tum-nal feast!

MEN.—Tenor. (8ve lower)
O let the gales of grey-ey'd morn - ing, The ge - nial sun and ev'ning
Bass.
O let the gales of grey-ey'd morn - ing, The ge - nial sun and ev'ning
fz
fz
fz
WOMEN.—1st Treble.
The ev'ning
2nd Treble.
The ev'ning
Alto.
The ev'ning
show'r,
show'r,
dol.
fz
show'r, and ge-nial sun With pow'r pro - duc - tive bless the land.
Tutti.
The hopes of
Alto. Tutti.
show'r, and ge-nial sun With pow'r pro - duc - tive bless the land.
The hopes of
Tenor. Tutti.
show'r, and ge-nial sun With pow'r pro - duc - tive bless the land.
The hopes of
Bass. Tutti.
The hopes of

man, . . the hopes of man shall then be crown'd, ...
man, . . the hopes of man shall then be crown'd, ...
man, . . the hopes of man shall then be crown'd, ...
man, the hopes of man shall then be crown'd, . . .
C
un poco più moto. ♩ = 100.
and songs of joy Thy praise shall tell.
and songs of joy Thy praise shall tell. With pow'r pro - duc - tive, with pow'r pro -
and songs of joy Thy praise shall tell.
and songs of joy Thy praise shall tell.
C
un poco piu moto.
With pow'r pro - duc - tive, with pow'r pro - duc - tive, with pow'r pro -
duc - tive bless the land, with pow'r pro - duc - tive bless the
With pow'r pro -

- duc - - tive bless the land, bless the land, bless the
land, bless . . . the land, . . . bless the land,
With pow'r pro - duc - tive, with pow'r pro -
- duc - tive, with pow'r pro - duc - tive, with pow'r pro - duc - - tive bless the
fz
land, with pow'r pro - duc - tive, with pow'r pro - duc - tive bless the
with pow'r pro - duc - tive, with pow'r pro - duc - tive bless the
- duc - tive, bless the land, with pow'r pro -
land, with pow'r pro - duc - tive, with pow'r pro - duc - tive bless the
fz
fz
D
land, bless . . the land,
land, with pow'r pro - duc - tive bless the
- duc - tive, with pow'r pro - duc - tive, with pow'r pro - duc - tive bless the
land, with pow'r pro - duc - tive, with pow'r pro -
fz
D

with pow'r pro - duc - tive, with pow'r pro - duc - tive bless
land, . . with pow'r pro - duc - tive
land, the land, bless the land, bless the
- duc - tive bless the land, bless the land, bless
the land, the land, with pow'r pro - duc - tive, with
bless the land, with pow'r . . pro - duc - -
land, the land, with pow'r pro - duc - tive, with
the land, with pow'r pro - duc - tive, with
pow'r pro - duc - tive, with pow'r pro - duc - tive, with pow'r pro -
- tive, with pow'r pro - duc - tive, with pow'r pro - duc - tive, with pow'r pro -
pow'r pro - duc - tive bless the land, with pow'r pro - duc - tive, with pow'r pro -
pow'r pro - duc - tive bless the land, with pow'r pro - duc - tive bless the

E

- duc - tive, with pow'r pro - duc - tive bless the land; The hopes of

- duc - tive, with pow'r pro - duc - tive bless the land, bless the

- duc - tive, with pow'r pro - duc - tive bless the land; The hopes of

land, bless the land; The hopes of man . . shall then be

E

fz *fz* *fz*

man shall then be crown'd, the hopes, the hopes of

land; . . The hopes of man shall then be

man shall then be crown'd,

crown'd, shall then be crown'd, shall be crown'd,

ff *fz*

man . . shall then be crown'd,

crown'd, shall then be crown'd,

f And songs of joy Thy praise shall

f shall be crown'd, And songs of joy Thy praise, Thy praise shall

f *fz*

f
And songs of joy Thy praise, Thy praise shall tell, Thy praise, Thy
f
And songs of joy Thy praise, Thy praise shall tell, Thy praise, Thy praise shall
tell, Thy praise . . shall tell;
tell, Thy praise . . shall tell; And songs of joy Thy praise, Thy praise shall
fz
sf
sf
praise . . shall tell, . . shall tell, . .
tell, ... Thy praise . . shall tell, . .
And songs of . . joy Thy praise shall tell,
tell, And songs of . . joy Thy praise shall tell, . .
fz
F
ff
And songs of joy Thy praise, Thy praise shall tell, Thy praise shall tell, Thy
ff
And songs of joy Thy praise, Thy praise shall tell, Thy praise shall tell, Thy
ff
And songs of joy Thy praise, Thy praise shall tell, Thy praise shall tell, Thy
ff
And songs of joy Thy praise, Thy praise shall tell, Thy praise shall tell, Thy
F
ff
fz
fz
ff

praise, ... Thy praise
shall . . . . . .
praise . . . .
shall . . . . . .
praise . . . .
shall . . . . . .
praise, ... Thy praise
shall . . . . . .
Ped.
Ped.
tell.
p
And songs of
tell.
And songs of
tell.
And songs of
tell.
And songs of
pp
Ped.
Ped.
f
joy . . Thy praise . . . .
shall tell.
joy Thy praise . . . .
shall tell.
joy . . Thy praise . . . .
shall tell,
joy . . Thy praise . . . .
shall tell.
8va.
loco.
ff
Ped.

No. 8. RECIT AND AIR.—"OUR FERVENT PRAYERS ARE HEARD."

No. 9. DUET AND CHORUS.—"SPRING, HER LOVELY CHARMS UNFOLDING."

May. Come, com - pan- ions, let us wan-der, let us wan - der

'mid the sweets of May.

A JANE.

Spring, her lovely charms unfolding,

Spring, her lovely charms unfolding,

A

Calls us to the fields; Spring, her lovely charms un - fold-ing, Calls us,

Calls us to the fields; Spring, her lovely charms un - fold-ing, Calls us,

calls . . us, calls us to the fields. Come, sweet maid-ens,

calls us, calls us to the fields.

let us wan-der, let us wan-der
Come com-pa-nions, let . us wan-der, let us wan-der
O'er the fra-grant scene. Spring her love-ly charms un-fold-ing, Calls us,
O'er the fra-grant scene. Spring her love-ly charms un-fold-ing, Calls us,
calls . . . . . . us to the fields.
calls . . . . . . us to the fields.
JANE.
Let us gai-ly tread the dewdrops, Cull,
pp
rf

cull the bloom-ing flow'rs.
LUCAS.
See the valleys, see the meadows, Where the
li-lies sip the stream-let!
B
SOPRANO. CHORUS.
Spring, her lovely charms un-
GIRLS. ALTO. CHORUS.
Spring, her love - - -
1st TENOR. CHORUS.
Spring, her lovely charms un-
2nd TENOR. CHORUS.
Spring, her lovely charms un-
- - fold-ing, calls us, calls us, calls us to the fields,
- - ly charms un - fold - ing, calls us to the fields,
- - fold-ing, calls us, calls . . . us to the fields.
- - fold-ing, calls us, calls us, calls us, to the fields,

Tutti. Soprano.
Let us wan-der o'er the fra - - - - - - - - grant,
Tutti. Alto.
Let us wan-der o'er the fra-grant scene, the
Tutti. Tenor.
Let us wan-der o'er the
Tutti. Bass.
Let us wan-der
fra - - grant scene. Spring, her love-ly charms un-fold-ing, Calls us,
fra - - - - grant scene. Spring, her love-ly charms un-fold-ing, Calls us,
fra - - grant scene. Spring, her love-ly charms un-fold-ing, Calls us,
o'er the fra-grant scene. Spring, her love-ly charms un-fold-ing, Calls us,
calls . . . . us to the fields.
calls . . . . us to the fields.
calls . . . . us to the fields.
calls . . . . us to the fields.
dim.
Ped.

JANE.
Mark the mountains! see the wa-ters! View the lu-cid
LUCAS.
sky! All is love-ly, all de-light-ful, All . . re-plete, re-plete . . with
sempre p
JANE.
joy! See the play-ful lamb-kins
f
ff
p
bound-ing!
LUCAS.
Fish in sport the wa ters
cleav - ing!
JANE.
Bees from
cres.
p
pp

LUCAS.
flow'r to flow'r are fly - ing.
Tune - ful
sempre pp
birds thro' branch-es flut - ter.
C
TUTTI.
All is love - ly, all de - light - ful, all re-
All is.. love - ly, all de - light - ful, all re-
ff
- plete, re - plete with joy.
GIRLS.
O what plea - sure,
p

What en - joy - ment, Fills our grate - ful hearts!
What en - joy - ment, Fills our grate - ful hearts!
YOUTHS. SOPRANO.
O what glad - ness, O what rapture, Reigns . . with - in the
TENOR.
O what glad - ness, O what rapture, Reigns . . with - in the
sempre legato.
breast!
SIMON.
breast! Till the feel - ings. all ec -
sempre piano
e legato.
- sta - tic, all ec - sta - tic, Own a pres - ent, a
f p f p f p fz
f p

GIRLS AND YOUTHS.
D
TUTTI.
With our prais - es
TUTTI.
With our prais - es
TUTTI.
With our prais - es
pres - ent God.
p
grate - - ful flow - ing, grate - - ful flow - ing, magni -
grate - - ful flow - ing, grate - ful flow - ing, magni -
grate - - ful flow - ing, grate - - ful flow - ing, magni -
- fy His Name!
- fy His Name!
- fy His Name! Let the voice of pure thanks-giv - ing Rise a -
f
Let the voice of pure thanks-giv - ing Rise a -
f

E Tutti. *f*
Let the

Tutti. *f*
Let the

- bove the clouds.
Tutti. *f*
Let the

- bove the clouds.
Tutti. *f*
Let the

E
ff

voice of pure thanks-giv - ing Rise a - bove the

voice of pure thanks-giv - ing Rise a - bove . . . the

voice of pure thanks - giv - ing Rise a - bove . . . the

voice of pure thanks-giv - ing Rise a - bove the

clouds.

clouds.

clouds.

clouds.

p

No. 10. CHORUS.—"GOD OF LIGHT."

Also published in Novello's Tonic Sol-fa Series, No. 1774.

Solo.
stores The earth with plenty flows,
And whose Almighty
Tutti.
Solo.
stores The earth with plenty flows,
God . . of life! And whose Almighty
Tutti. f
Solo.
stores The earth with plenty flows,
God . . of life! And whose Almighty
p
ff
pp
love . . Makes glad the heart of man.
Hail, gracious Lord!
love . . Makes glad the heart of man.
Hail, gracious Lord!
love . . Makes glad the heart of man.
Hail, gracious Lord!
p
Tutti. f
Hail, gracious Lord, God . . of light! God . . of life! Hail, gracious
Tutti. f
God . . of light! God . . of life! Hail, gracious
Tutti. f
Hail, gracious Lord, God . . of light! God . . of life! Hail, gracious
Tutti.
f
Hail, gracious Lord, God . . of light! God . . of life! Hail, gracious
fp
fp
fp
fp

JANE.
Lord!
Hail . . gracious Lord!
Lord!
LUCAS.
Lord!
God . . of life!
SIMON.
Lord!
God . . of light!
A Allegro. 𝅗𝅥 = 104.
End-less praise to
End-less praise to thee we'll sing, Al - - mighty
End-less praise to thee we'll sing, Al - - mighty Lord of all.
A
Allegro.
8ves.
End-less praise to thee we'll sing, Al - mighty Lord . of all, Al -
thee we'll sing, Al - - mighty Lord of all. End - less praise
Lord of all, End-less praise to thee we'll sing
Endless praise to thee we'll sing Al -
8ves.

- - mighty Lord, . . . Almigh - ty Lord of all! End - less
end - less praise to Thee we'll sing, Al - mighty Lord of all!
Almighty Lord of all! End - less praise to Thee we'll sing, Al -
- - mighty Lord of all! Al - mighty Lord! Al -
fz
fz
fz
praise to Thee we'll sing, Al - mighty Lord of
End - less praise, end - less praise . . . to . . Thee we'll
- - mighty Lord . . of all, End - less praise to
- migh - ty Lord . . of all! End -
all! Al - mighty Lord of all! Al - mighty Lord! End - less
sing, Al - mighty Lord of all! Endless praise to Thee we'll sing, End-
Thee we'll sing, End - less praise, end - less praise, end - less praise,
- less praise to Thee we'll sing, End - less praise, end - less praise, end-
fz
fz
fz
fz

fz
fz
praise to Thee we'll sing, Al - - mighty Lord, Al - - mighty
fz
- - less praise . . . to Thee . . . we'll sing, Al - - mighty Lord . . .
fz
Al-migh-ty Lord, to Thee we'll sing Almighty
fz
fz
- - less praise . . . to Thee . . . we'll sing, Al - - mighty Lord, Lord
sf
fz
sf
sf
sf
B
Lord of all! Lord of all! Almigh-ty Lord, Lord of
. . . of all! Lord of all! Almigh-ty Lord, Lord of
Lord! Lord of all! Almigh-ty Lord, Lord of
. . . . of all! Lord of all! To Thee we'll sing, Al - - mighty Lord,
B
fz
all! Lord of all! Al - mighty Lord, Lord of all! Almigh-ty
all! Lord . . of all! Al - mighty Lord, Lord of all! Almigh-ty
all! Lord . . of all! Al - mighty Lord, Lord of all! Almigh-ty
Lord . . of all! Al - mighty Lord, Lord of all! Almigh-ty
fz

Lord, Al - mighty Lord, Al - migh - ty Lord . . . of all!
Lord, Al - mighty Lord, Al - mighty Lord . . . of all!
Lord, Al - mighty Lord, Al - mighty Lord! End -
Lord, Al - mighty Lord of all, Lord . . of all!
fz
fz
fz
fz
C
End - less praise to Thee we'll sing, Al -
End-less praise to Thee we'll
- less praise to Thee we'll sing, End - less praise to Thee . . we'll
End-less praise to Thee we'll sing, end-less
C
fz
fz
ff
- mighty Lord of all! Al - mighty Lord of all!
sing, Al - migh - - ty Lord of all! Lord, Lord of all!
sing, Al - migh - - - ty Lord of all!
praise to Thee we'll sing, Al - migh - ty Lord of all,

End - less praise, end - - - less praise we'll sing,
End - less praise, end - less praise to Thee, to Thee we'll sing,
End - less, end - less praise to Thee, to Thee we'll sing,
End - less praise to Thee we'll sing,
fz
fz
p
End - less praise, end - - - less praise we'll sing. God of light!
End - less praise, end - less praise to Thee, to Thee we'll sing. God of light!
End - less, end - less praise to Thee, to Thee we'll sing. God of light!
End - less praise to Thee we'll sing, God of light!
pp
f
ff
God of life!
D
Hail, . . gracious Lord!
Hail, . .
God of life!
God of life!
God of life!
ten.

f
. . gracious Lord! Hail, . . gracious Lord! Hail, . .
End - - less praise to Thee we'll
Hail, . . gracious Lord! Hail, . . gracious Lord!
Hail, gracious Lord! Hail, gracious Lord! Hail, gracious
fz
. . gracious Lord! gracious Lord! gracious Lord!
sing. Hail, gracious Lord! gracious Lord!
Hail, gracious Lord! gracious Lord!
Lord, Hail, gracious Lord! gracious Lord!
ff
E
End - - less praise . . .
End - - less praise to Thee we'll sing, . . .
End - - - - - - less praise, End - less
End - less praise, End - less praise,

ff
to Thee we'll sing, Al - mighty
to Thee we'll sing, Al - mighty
praise . . to Thee we'll sing, Al - mighty
to Thee, to Thee we'll sing, Al - mighty
fz
ff
Lord of all, . . . Lord of all! Lord, Lord of
fz
Ped.
all! Lord, . . . Lord of all! . . . .
fz
Ped.
END OF SPRING.

SUMMER.

No. 11. RECIT.—"HER FACE IN DEWY VEIL CONCEAL'D."

To gloomy caves repair
The black ill-omen'd birds of night;
And with their mournful cries
No more the tim-id
heart appal.
p
pp
fz
sempre pp
SIMON.—BASS.
The crest-ed har-bin-ger of day
With
p
fz
pp

live-ly note the shepherd wakes, Who from his cottage hies, The freshness of the morn to taste.
f
No. 12. Air.—"FROM OUT THE FOLD THE SHEPHERD DRIVES."
Allegretto. ♩. = 84.
p
SIMON.
From out the fold the shepherd drives His bleat-ing flock and low-ing herd, . .
p
To browse a-long the ver-dant hill, Dew - drops shak - ing
to . . the ground, a - long the ver - - dant hill, Dew - drops

shak - ing to . . the ground.
He stands, and ga - zes towards the east, And
on his staff in si - lence leans, . .
And on his staff in si - - -
- - lence leans, Un - til the pow'r- ful king of day Glorious darts his beams . . a
- round,
Glo-rious darts
. his beams,
darts his beams a - round
a

- round, darts his beams, . . darts . . his beams a-round.

pp f p f

p cres. f

No. 13. Recit.—"LO! NOW ASLANT THE DEW-BRIGHT EARTH."

JANE.

Voice.

Lo! now aslant the dew-bright earth, In boundless majesty,

Accomp.

♩ = 69.

f

in boundless majes-ty he looks! And o'er the mountains,

p p

tow'rs, and wand'ring streams, Resplendent glowing, spreads ethereal gold.

f

No. 14 TRIO AND CHORUS.—"BEHOLD ON HIGH HE MOUNTS."

A
Allegro. 𝅗𝅥 = 104.
Hail, thou glo - - rious sun! Thou source of light and life, all
Hail, thou glo - - rious sun! Thou source of light and life, all
Hail, thou glo - - rious sun! Thou source of light and life, all
Hail, thou glo - - rious sun! Thou source of light and life, all
A
Allegro.
hail! Hail, thou glo - rious sun! Sub - lime and u - ni - ver-sal orb, Sub-
hail! Hail, thou glo - rious sun! Sub - lime and u - ni - ver-sal orb, Sub-
hail! Hail, thou glo - rious sun! Sub-lime and u - ni -
hail! Hail, thou glo - rious sun! Sub-lime and u - ni -
- lime and u - ni - ver - sal orb, This earth's pervading soul, per - va - ding soul, Cre -
- lime and u - ni - ver - sal orb, This earth's pervading soul, per - va - ding soul, Cre -
- ver - sal, u - ni - ver - sal orb, This earth's pervading soul, . . . per - va - ding soul,
- ver - sal, u - ni - ver - sal orb, This earth's per - va - ding, per - va - ding soul,

- a - tion, cre - a - - tion cries, . . all hail, this earth's per - va - - ding
- a - tion, cre - a - - tion cries, all hail, this earth's per - va - ding, per - va - ding
Cre - a - - tion cries, all hail, this earth's per - va - - - - ding
Cre-a-tion cries, all hail, this earth's per - va - ding
fz
soul, Cre - a - tion, cre - a - - - - - tion cries, all hail!
soul, Cre - a - tion, cre - a - tion, cre - a - tion cries, all hail!
soul, Cre - a - tion, cre - a - tion cries, all hail!
soul, Cre - a - tion, cre - a - tion cries, all hail!
fz
p
JANE.
Who can express the pure de - light
LUCAS.
Who can express the pure de - light
SIMON.
Who can express the pure de - light

Thy cheerful presence yields to man? Or who recount, re - count the
Thy cheerful presence yields to man? Or who re - count
Thy cheerful presence yields to man? Or who re - count the good,
pp
B
Chorus.—Tutti.
might - y good That from thy rays . . . the earth re - ceives? Who
Tutti.
Who
Tutti.
the might - y good That from thy rays the earth re - ceives? Who
Tutti.
re - count the might-y good That from thy rays the earth re - ceives? Who
B
f
can ex - press the pure delight Thy cheer-ful pre - sence yields to man? The
can ex - press the pure delight Thy cheer-ful pre - sence yields to man? The
can ex - press the pure delight Thy cheer-ful pre - sence yields to man? The
can ex - press the pure delight Thy cheer-ful pre - sence yields to man? The

Andante. ♩= 56.
JANE.
pure delight Who can express? Who? Who?
Thy ge - nial warmth gives
pure delight Who can express? Who? Who?
pure delight Who can express? Who? Who?
pure delight Who can express? Who? Who?
Andante.
p
health and joy;
LUCAS.
Thy ge - nial warmth gives health and joy;
SIMON.
Thy ge - nial warmth gives
But un - - to God Himself we owe The pow'r thy
But un - - to God Himself we owe The pow'r thy
health and joy; But un - - to God Himself we owe The pow'r thy
fz
pp
fp

C
Tutti. Allegro. ♩= 104.
beams dis - play, The pow'r thy beams dis - play.
Tutti. Hail! thou glo - rious
beams . . dis - play, The pow'r thy beams dis - play.
Tutti. Hail! thou glo - rious
beams . . dis - play, The pow'r thy beams dis - play.
Hail! thou glo - rious
Allegro.
fp
ff
fz
sun! Thou source of light and life, all hail! Hail! thou glorious
sun! Let shouts of joy re - sound thy name throughout the world, Thy
sun! Let shouts of joy re - sound thy name throughout the world,
sun! Let shouts of joy re- sound thy name throughout the

D
name . . . . throughout the
let shouts of joy . . resound thy name, thy name, thy name, thy
world, let shouts . . . .
world, let
D
fz
fz
world, let shouts . . . .
name . . . . . throughout the world, let . . shouts . . of
. . . . of joy re-sound thy name through-out, throughout the
shouts . . . . of joy, . .
fz
fz
. . . . of joy re-sound thy name, re - sound thy name throughout the
joy, . . of joy re-sound thy name, thy name throughout the
world, let shouts of joy re-sound thy name, re - sound thy name,
let shouts . . . . of
fz
fz

world, thy name . . . . throughout the world, thy
world, thy name . . . . throughout the world,
thy name, ... thy name throughout the world, thy
joy re - sound thy name, thy name throughout the world,
fz fz

E JANE.
name, thy name, thy name throughout the world, thy name . . . . . .
thy name, thy name throughout the world,
LUCAS.
name, thy name, thy name throughout the world, thy name . . . .
SIMON.
thy name, thy name throughout the world, thy name . . . .
E
fz fz p

. . . . throughout the
. . . . . . thy name . . . . throughout the
. . . . throughout the

TUTTI.
JANE.
world, thy name, thy name, thy name throughout the world, thy
TUTTI.
thy name, thy name throughout the world,
TUTTI.
LUCAS.
world, thy name, thy name, thy name throughout the world, thy
TUTTI.
world, thy name, thy name throughout the world,
f
fz
fz
fz
Name,
TUTTI.
thy name, thy name, thy name, thy name throughout the world, thy
ff
TUTTI.
thy name, thy name, thy name throughout the world, thy
ff
Name,
TUTTI.
thy name, thy name throughout the world, thy
ff
TUTTI.
thy name, thy name throughout the world, thy
ff
fz
fz
fz
fz
ff
name throughout the world.
name throughout the world.
name throughout the world.
name throughout the world.
3
3

No. 15. Recit.—"NOW SWARMS THE VILLAGE O'ER THE MEAD."
SIMON.
Voice.
Accomp.
Now swarms the village o'er the mead, The rus-tic youth, the rud-dy maid; The breath-ing har - vest spreads a-round, Whose fra-grance scents the air; From dale to dale, wak-ing the breeze, re-sounds the voice of hap-py la - bour, of jo-cund mirth, and so - cial glee.
fz
f
p
No. 16. Recit.—"'TIS NOON, AND NOW DIRECT THE SUN."
LUCAS.
'Tis noon, and now di-rect the sun darts down his rays. O'er
pp

heav'n and earth the eye beholds
His forceful blaze
resistless outspread.
f
p
Moderato. ♩= 66.
From pole
to pole,
o'er
Moderato. A tempo.
legato.
cleaving fields
Of a-rid herbs and wi-ther'd flow'rs,
A dazzling deluge reigns.
No. 17.
Cavatina.—"DISTRESSFUL NATURE FAINTING SINKS"
Largo.
Voice.
Accomp.
♪= 72.
pp
pp

LUCAS.
Distress - ful na - ture fainting sinks. Droop-ing leaf-age, Thirst - y
pas-tures, Founts exhaust - ed, Show the ty - rant rage of heat; And
pant - ing lan-guish man and beast, Out-stretch'd up-on the
ground, outstretch'd upon the ground. Distress - ful na- ture fainting sinks! Drooping
leaf - age, Thirsty pastures, Founts ex-haust-ed, Show the ty - rant rage of
fp
f
p
sempre p
legato.

heat; And pant - ing, and pant - ing languish man and
f
p
beast, Out - stretch'd, out - stretch'd up-on the ground, And
sempre p
panting, and panting lan - guish man and beast, outstretch'd up - on the
pp
ground, . . Outstretch'd up - on the ground.
Legato.
cres.
f
p
pp

Recit.—"O WELCOME NOW"

Poco Adagio. ♩ = 56.

mez.

JANE. (Treble.)

p pp p

O wel-come now, ye groves and bow'rs! Ye lofty pines, ye a-ged oaks! Whose branches lend a cooling shade; And

sweet-ly to the list-'ning ear
ten
pp
pp
In mur - murs whisp'ring speak.
pp
3
3
p
O'er dow-ny moss the purling brook
p
3
3
Its li-quid sil-ver rolls;
pp

And 'neath the shade, with sooth-ing hum,
pp
The sport-ive in-sects play.
The
f
p
balm-y scent of fragrant herbs
On zephyr's wing is
p
pp
borne,
and from the ev'ning bow'r is
heard
The shepherd's tune-ful lay.
p
ra - len - tan - do.
f

No. 19. AIR.—"O HOW PLEASING TO THE SENSES."

- - vades, . . . per - vades Th' in - vi - go-ra - ted frame.
O how pleas - ing to the sen - ses Comes the
sweet and cool - ing breeze!
Beams the
sempre legato.
eye with joy ex - pand - ed, As the stream of life, the
stream of life per - vades Th' in - vi - go - ra - ted, th' in -

Allegro assai. ♩ = 144.
- - vi - go - rat - ed frame.
Allegro assai.
p
De - light up - lifts the heart, And fan - cy's ma - gic
p
cres.
pow'r, and fan - - - - - - - - - cy's ma - gic pow'r
f fz p
fz
O'er na - ture bears the
fz p
soul On sweet . . en - chant - ed wing;
fz p

O'er na - ture bears the soul On sweet, on sweet, on sweet en -
- chant-ed wing; O'er na - - - - - - - - - - - - - - - - - - -
- - ture bears the soul, On sweet, on sweet en - chant - ed
wing. De-light up-lifts the heart, And

fan - cy's ma - gic pow'r O'er na - ture bears the soul On
sweet en - chant - ed wing, On
sweet en - chant-ed wing, . . en-chant
ed, en - chant ed
wing.
f
p
fz
p
f
p

No. 20. Recit.—"BEHOLD! SLOW SETTLING O'ER THE LURID GROVE.'

Adagio.
By fear - ful man for - got: Th'a - erial tribes descend; The clouds low roll-ing
Adagio.
on pre-pare the e - - le -men - tal strife.
Poco Adagio. ♩= 60
Poco Adagio.
sempre pp
sempre staccato.
JANE.
Through all the dun expanse A
bod - ing si-lence reigns: With - out a
Ped.
pp
breath The for-est shakes, And na - ture seems to ru - in doom'd.
Attacca subito.

No. 21. CHORUS.—"HARK! THE DEEP TREMENDOUS VOICE."

aw - ful thun - der roars! The
aw - ful thun - der roars! The
aw - ful thun - der roars! The
aw - ful thun - der roars! The
fz p fz p fz p
tem - pest howls a - round; a - way, a -
tem - pest howls a - round; a - way, a -
tem - pest howls a - round; a - way,
tem - pest howls a - round; a - way,
fz p ff
- way; ah, let us fly.
- way; ah, let . . us fly.
a - way;
a - way;

A
A-way! ah
Flash - - - - - es of liv - id flame Dart thro' the
Flash - - - - - - es of liv - id flame Dart thro' the
Flash - es of liv - id flame Dart thro' the air,
A
fz fz fz fz
let us fly; A - way!
air, . . . And from the burst - ing clouds the
air, And from the burst - ing clouds the
And from the burst - ing clouds the
fz fz
Heav'n pro - tect us!
flood In am - - ple tor - - rents
flood . . . In am - - ple tor - - rents
flood , . . In am - - ple tor - - rents

B
Heav'n pro
pours, In am - - ple tor - - - - rents pours.
pours, In am - - ple tor - - - - rents pours.
pours, In am - - ple tor - - - - rents pours.
B
p
- tect us! Heav'n pro - tect us!
Dread - - ful
Dread - - ful
Dread - - ful
ff
Heav'n pro - tect us!
rage the winds; The sky is all in
rage the winds; The sky is all in
rage the winds; The sky is all in

Heav'n pro - tect us!
flames, . . . The sky is all in flames; . . .
flames, The sky is all in flames; . . .
flames, . . . The sky is all in flames;
O what hor - ror!
C
Peal on peal, with
Peal on
Peal on peal, with
fz
fz
O what hor - ror! O God!
fear - ful crash, with fear - ful, fear - ful crash, Con - vuls - ing
peal, with fear - - - ful crash, Con -vuls - ing
fear - ful crash, with fear - ful, fear - ful crash, Con- vuls - ing
fz
fz
fz

O
God!
heav'n, the thun - der rolls!
Peal on peal, with fear - ful
heav'n, the thun - der rolls!
Peal on peal, with fear - ful
heav'n, the thun - der rolls!
Peal on peal, with fear - ful
fz
p
pp
ff
O what hor - ror! O what hor-ror!
crash,
Con - vuls - ing heav'n, the thun - der rolls!
crash,
Con - vuls - ing heav'n, the thun - der rolls!
crash,
Con - vuls - ing heav'n, the thun - der rolls!
D
Allegro. 𝅗𝅥 = 132
O
God!
O
God!
The
D
Allegro.

O God!
The firm and
firm and deep found-a - tions Of earth it-self are mov'd; The firm and deep found-
The firm and
deep found - a - tions Of earth it - self are mov'd, of earth it - self . . . .
- - a - tions, the firm and deep found - a - tions Of earth it-self are mov'd;
O God!
deep found - a - tions Of earth it - self are mov'd. O
. . . . are mov'd, The firm and
The firm and deep found - a - tions.
The firm and deep found - a - tions of
fz

God! O what hor - ror!
deep . . found - a - tions . Of earth it - self . . are mov'd, of earth it-self are
O God! The firm and deep found-a - tions of
earth it - self are mov'd, of earth it - self are mov'd. of earth it - self . .
E
O God! Peal on peal, with fearful crash, Con-
mov'd. O God! Peal on peal, with fearful crash, Con-
earth . . . . . are mov'd. O what
. . . . are mov'd. Heav'n pro - tect us!
fz
- vuls-ing heav'n, the thunder rolls. O . . . God! The firm and
- vuls-ing heav'n, the thunder rolls. O . . . . God!
Hor - ror! O God! The firm and deep found-
Peal on peal, ... with fear - ful crash, with fear - ful
fz

deep found - a - tions Of earth it - self are mov'd, of earth it - self are
The firm and deep found - a - tions Of earth it - self are mov'd, of
- - a - tions, the firm and deep found - a - tions Of earth it - self are mov'd, of
crash! The firm deep found - a - tions Of earth it - self are mov'd,
fz
mov'd, of earth it - self are mov'd, of earth . . it - self, ...
earth it - self are mov'd, of earth it - self are mov'd, of earth it - self, . . of
earth it - self are mov'd, of earth . . it - self . . are mov'd, The firm and
The firm and
ff
. . . . of earth it - self are
earth it - self are mov'd, of earth it - self are
deep found-a - tions Of earth, of earth it - self are
deep found-a - tions Of earth, of earth . . it - self are

F
mov'd!
O God!
O . . . .
mov'd!
O God!
O .
mov'd!
O God!
O . . . .
mov'd!
O God!
O
F
ten.
ten.
ff
fz
fff
Ped.
*
God! . . .
The
God! . .
The
God! . . .
The
God! . . .
The
dim.
p
pp
sempre p
firm and deep found - a - - tions Of earth it - self are
firm and deep found - a - - tions Of earth it - self are
firm and deep found - a - - tions Of earth it - self are
firm and deep found - a - - tions Of earth it - self are
cres.
f

G
pp
mov'd; The firm and deep found - a - tions of
mov'd; The firm and deep found - a - tions of
mov'd; The firm and deep found - a - tions of
mov'd; The firm and deep found - a - tions of
earth it - self . . . are mov'd.
earth it - self are mov'd.
earth it - self . . . are mov'd.
earth it - self are mov'd.
sempre pp
dim.
ppp
pp

No. 22 TRIO AND CHORUS.—"NOW CEASE THE CONFLICTS."

robe . . . of joy;
SIMON.
His flock se-cure, the shep-herd hies Light-heart - ed, light-
- heart-ed to his home; Light-hearted to his home;
LUCAS.
The
quail with clamour calls her mate;
JANE.
A-round the hidden crickets
chirp;
SIMON.
While croak the frogs with-in the
fz
p
pp

pool;
JANE.
And tolls the ev'ning bell, And tolls the ev'ning bell. . .
LUCAS.
And tolls the ev'ning bell, And tolls the ev'ning bell. . .
SIMON.
And tolls the ev'ning bell, And tolls the ev'ning bell. . .
Allegro. 𝅗𝅥 = 144.
Now shines the glit - t'ring host of stars:
Allegro.
Now shines the glit - t'ring host of stars:
Allegro.
Now shines the glit - t'ring host of stars:
Allegro.
dolce.

The hour of sweet re - pose is near.
The hour of sweet re - pose is near.
The hour of sweet re - pose is near.
f
f
TENOR. TUTTI.
A
Wel-come, Wel-come, gen - tle
BASS. TUTTI.
Wel-come, Wel-come, gen - tle
A
sleep! Sooth-ing balm of ev' - ry care!
sleep! Sooth-ing balm of ev' - ry care!
fz
O thou that in the cot of toil Dost quick - ly
O thou that in the cot of toil Dost quick - ly
fz
fz
fz
fz

close the lids of health! Welcome, welcome, gentle
close the lids of health! Welcome, welcome, gentle
B
Treble. Tutti.
sleep, To rest, to rest, to rest, a-way!
Alto. Tutti.
sleep, To rest, to rest, to rest, a-way!
fz
fz
p
Treble.
The ev'-ning bell a-gain has
Alto.
The ev'-ning bell a-gain has
Tenor.
The ev'-ning bell a-gain has
Bass.
The ev'-ning bell a-gain has

toll'd; The wink - ing stars to sleep in - vite; The
toll'd; The wink - ing stars to sleep in - vite; The
toll'd; The wink - ing stars to sleep in - vite; The
toll'd; The wink - ing stars to sleep in - vite; The
C
hour of sweet re - pose is near. To rest, to
hour of sweet re - pose is near. To rest, to
hour of sweet re - pose is near. Welcome, Welcome,
hour of sweet re - pose is near. Welcome, Welcome,
C
rest, a - way; to rest, a - way!
rest, a - way; to rest, a - way!
gen - tle sleep, gen - tle sleep!
gen - tle sleep, gen - tle sleep!

The ev' - ning bell a - gain has
The ev' - ning bell a - gain has
The ev' - ning bell a - gain has
The ev' - ning bell a - gain has
toll'd: The wink - ing stars to sleep . . . . in -
toll'd: The wink - ing stars, The wink - ing stars to
toll'd: The wink - ing stars to sleep in - vite, to sleep . . . .
toll'd: The wink - ing stars to sleep in - vite; . . .
- vite; . . . . To rest, to rest, . . to
sleep in - vite; . . . . . To rest, to rest, . . to
. . . . in - vite; . . . . . To rest, to rest, . . to
. . . . To rest, to rest, . . to
D

END OF SUMMER

AUTUMN.

No. 23. OVERTURE.

No. 24. RECIT.—"WHATE'ER THE BLOSSOM'D SPRING."

No. 25. TERZETTO AND CHORUS.—THUS NATURE, EVER KIND.

wealth, With Au - tumn's wealth she pays, . . she rich - ly

pays, With Au - - tumn's wealth . . . she rich-ly pays.

JANE.

O In - - dus - try, how rich . . thy

LUCAS.

O In - - dus - try, how rich . . thy

gifts! The cot - tage where we dwell, Our clothing and our

gifts! The cot - tage where we dwell, Our clothing and our

food, Health, plenty, and con - tent, . . Are bless - - ings all . . by

food, Health, plenty, and con - tent, . . Are bless - - ings all . by

thee be - stow'd, Are bless - - ings all . . by thee . be -
thee . be - stow'd, Are bless - - ings all by thee . be -
SIMON.
All
- stow'd; All hail, O In - dus - try! From thee, from
- stow'd; All hail, . O In - dus - try! From thee, from
hail, ... all hail, O In - dus - try! From thee, from
fz
thee springs ev' - - ry good, from thee springs ev' - - ry
thee springs ev' - - ry good, from thee springs ev' - ry
thee springs ev' - - ry good, from thee springs ev' - ry

JANE.
good.
Each form of
good.
good.
vir - tuous life
fz
Through thee a - lone per - fec - tion
p
LUCAS.
gains;
Thy sim - - ple laws from vice de -
- fend . . . . .
The err - ing heart of man,
f
SIMON.
And fix his wand'ring steps
Ped.
*
p
sempre.
p

In paths, . . In paths of truth and

JANE.

LUCAS. From thee, from thee springs ev' - ry good!

From thee . . springs ev' - ry good!

SIMON.

pi - ous love. From thee . . springs ev' - ry good!

fz

From thee, from thee springs ev' - ry, ev' - ry

From thee, from thee . springs ev' - ry, ev' - ry

From thee, from thee springs ev' - ry, ev' ry

dim. *p*

Tutti.

good! All hail, O In-dus-try! From

Tutti.

All hail, . . O In - dus-try! From

Tutti.

good! All hail, all hail, O In - dus - try! From thee,

Tutti.

good! All hail, ... all hail, O In - dus-try! From thee.

f

thee, from thee, from thee springs ev' - - - ry
thee, from thee, from thee springs ev' - - - ry
from thee, from thee springs ev' - - ry, ev' - - - ry
from thee, from thee springs ev' - - ry, ev' - - ry
JANE.
good! The cottage where we dwell, Our clothing and our food, Health,
good!
LUCAS.
good! The cottage where we dwell, Our clothing and our food, Health,
SIMON.
good! The cottage where we dwell, Our clothing and our food, Health,
p
dol.
p
TUTTI.
plen-ty, and con-tent, Are bless - -ings all . . by thee . . be -
From
TUTTI.
From
TUTTI.
From
plen-ty, and con-tent, Are bless - -ings all . by thee . be -
plen-ty, and con-tent, Are bless - -ings all . . by thee be -
f

-stow'd. O In-dus-try, from thee, from thee springs
thee,
thee, from thee, from thee . . . springs ev'ry good, springs
thee, O In-dus-try, from thee springs . . . ev' . .
-stow'd.
TUTTI.
-stow'd. From thee, . . . O In-dus-try, from thee, from thee springs
fz
ev' - ry good! . . . .
ev' - ry good! . . .
- - ry good! . . . .
ev' - ry good! . . . .
f
Più Allegro. ♩= 108.
fz
fz
From thee, O In - dus -
fz
fz
From thee, O In - dus-try, from thee springs ev'-ry good! From
fz
fz
Più Allegro.
fz

From thee, O
fz
fz
From thee, O In - dus-try, from thee springs ev'ry good!
-try, from thee springs ev'ry good! From thee, From thee springs ev' - ry, ev'ry good!
thee, from thee, from thee, from thee springs ev' - ry, ev'ry good!
fz
fz
fz
In - dus- try, from thee springs ev' - ry good! From thee, O In - dus-
From thee, from thee springs ev' - ry, ev' - ry good!
From thee, from thee springs ev' - ry good! ev' - ry
fz
fz
From thee, O In - dus-try, from thee springs
fz
fz
fz
-try, from thee springs ev' - ry, ev' - ry, ev' - ry good! From
from thee springs ev' - ry, ev' - ry good! springs ev - - ry, ev'-ry good!
good! From thee, from thee, from thee springs ev'-ry good!
ev' - - ry good! From thee, from thee springs ev'-ry good! From

fz
thee, from thee springs ev' - - - - ry, ev'-ry good! springs ev'-ry
From thee, O In - dus-try, from thee springs ev'-ry good! from thee, from
From thee, O In - dus-try, springs ev' - ry good! from thee, from
thee, springs ev' - - - - - ry, good! from thee, from
good, springs ev' - ry good, from thee, from thee springs ev' - ry
thee springs ev' - - - - ry good! springs ev'-ry, ev' - ry good! From
thee springs ev' - ry, ev'-ry good! springs ev'-ry, ev' - ry good! From
thee springs ev' - ry good! from thee O In - dus - try, springs
good! From thee, from thee springs ev' - ry,
thee, O In - - dus - try, springs ev'ry, ev' - ry good! springs ev' - ry,
thee, O In - - dustry, springs ev - - - - - - ry good! From
ev'ry, ev' - - - ry, ev' - - - - - - ry good!

ev' - ry good! springs ev' - ry good, springs ev' - ry good! From
ev' - ry good! springs ev' - ry good, springs ev' - ry good! From thee,
thee springs ev' - ry, ev' - ry good! springs ev' - ry good! From thee,
From thee, O In - dus - try, springs ev' - - ry good! From -
fz
fz
thee springs ev' - ry, ev' - ry good! springs ev' - ry good, springs
from thee springs ev' - ry, ev' - ry good! springs ev' - -
from thee springs ev' - ry, ev' - ry good! From thee . . springs ev'ry, . . ev' - -
thee, from thee springs ev' - ry, ev' - - - - - - - - -
Org. Ped.
JANE.
ev' - - - ry, ev' - - ry good! The cot - tage where we
- - - - - - - ry, ev' - ry good!
LUCAS.
- - - ry, ev' - ry, ev' - ry good! The cot - tage where we
SIMON.
- - - - - - ry, ev' - ry, good! The cot - tage where we
p

Solo
Tutti. Solo. Tutti. Solo. Tutti.
dwell, Our cloth-ing and our food, Health, plen-ty, and con - tent, are
From thee, from thee, O In - dus -
Tutti. Tutti. Tutti.
From thee, from thee, O In - dus -
Tutti. Solo. Tutti. Solo. Tutti. Solo.
dwell, Our cloth-ing and our food, Health, plen-ty, and con - tent, are
From thee, from thee, O In - dus -
Tutti. Solo. Tutti. Solo. Tutti. Solo.
dwell, Our cloth-ing and our food, Health, plen-ty, and con - tent, are
From thee, from thee, O In - dus -
bless - ings all by thee, by thee be-stow'd,
- try, from thee, from thee springs ev' - ry, ev' - ry good!
- try, from thee, from thee springs ev' - ry, ev' - ry good!
bless - ings all by thee, by thee be-stow'd,
- try, from thee, from thee springs ev' - ry, ev' - ry good!
bless - ings all by thee, by thee be - stow'd,
- try, from thee, from thee springs ev' - ry, ev' - ry good!
Tutti. Solo. Tutti. Solo.
from thee springs ev' - ry good! from thee, from thee, from
from thee springs ev' - ry good! from . . . thee,
Tutti. Solo. Tutti. Solo.
from thee springs ev' - ry good! from thee, from thee, from
Solo. Tutti. Solo.
from thee springs ev' - ry good! from thee, from thee, from

TUTTI.
SOLO.
TUTTI.
thee, from thee, from thee springs ev' - - - - ry good, ev' - - - ry good. . . . . springs ev'ry good, ... springs ev'ry good!
from thee springs ev' - - - - ry good, ev' - - - ry good, ... springs ev'ry good, ... springs ev'ry good!
thee, from thee, from thee springs ev' - - ry good, ev' - - ry good, springs ev' - ry good, springs ev' - ry good!
thee, from thee, from thee springs ev' - - - - ry good, ev' - - ry good, springs ev'-ry, ev'ry good, springs ev'-ry, ev'ry good!
fz
ff
fz

No. 26. RECIT.—"YE SWAINS, NOW HASTEN."

No. 27. Duet.—"YE GAY AND PAINTED FAIR."

fair, . O come! And mark the simple child of truth! No tricks of art her charms de -
- form: Be - hold my Jane, my Jane be-hold! Be - hold my
Jane, be - hold! The bloom . of
youth ad - orns her cheek, Her smil - - ing eye beams
hap - pi-ness; And from . . her
f fz fz fz fz fz fz p
fz fz fz

lips breathes faith sin-cere, And from her lips breathes faith sin -

- cere, When love . . to me . . she vows, when love to

me . . she vows, when love to me . . she vows, when

love . . to me . . she vows.

JANE.

Ye

false and i - dle swains, a - way, a - way! Here lures of fraud are

spread in vain; And wi-ly tales of pas - sion feign'd
Ped.
Ped.
No list' - ning ear shall find. Ye i - - - -
- - dle swains, away! Here lures of fraud are spread in vain; And wi - ly tales of passion
feign'd No list' - ning, list'ning ear shall find, No list' - ning ear, . . no
list'-ning ear shall find. Mine eye no
f fz f fz fz fz p

gaudy dress en ti - ces; An ho - nest heart is what I prize:
Ful - fill'd . . are all my fondest
wishes, Ful - fill'd . . are all my fond-est wishes, Whilst
Lu - - - cas true . . re-mains, Whilst Lu-cas true re - mains, whilst
f
p
Lu-cas re - mains, ... whilst Lu - cas

true . . re - mains:
sempre p
LUCAS.
Leaves will fade and fall, Flow'rs and fruit de - cay,
Days and years e - lapse; Not so my constant love, Not
so my con - - - - - - - - - - - stant love.
fz
p
f
fz
JANE.
Green - er grows the leaf,
pp

Sweet-er breathes the flow'r,
Bright-er shines the
day,
When love lights up thine eye,
When
love . . . . lights
up . thine eye.
Adagio.
JANE.
What de-light! what de-
LUCAS.
What de-light! what de-
Adagio. ♩ = 60.
fz
p
f
fz

- light! where mutual fer - vour
Binds two hearts in fond af - fec - tion!
- light! where mutual fer - vour
Binds two hearts in fond af - fec - tion!
Death a - lone such bonds can break.
Death a - lone such bonds can break.
p
f
f
Ped.
What de - light! what de-light, where mutual
What de - light! what de-light, where mutual
p
fz
p
fz
p
*
fer - vour
Binds two hearts in fond af - fec - tion!
fer - vour
Binds two hearts in fond af - fec - tion!
pp

Death a - lone such bonds can break;
Death a - lone such bonds can break;
Dear-est
Ped.
Dear-est Lu-cas!
Allegro. ♩ = 104.
Love to faithful love res-pon-sive
maiden!
Allegro.
Love to faithful love res-pon-sive
Allegro.
Is the high - est pitch of rap-ture
Is the high - est pitch of rap-ture
Heav'n be-stows on mor - tal life. . .
Love to
Heav'n be-stows on mor - tal life. . .

faithful love res - pon - sive Is the highest pitch of rap - ture
Love, . . to faithful love res - pon - sive Is the highest pitch of rap - ture
Heav'n be - stows on mor - tal life;
Heaven be - stows on mor - tal life;
Dear - est Lu - cas! Dear - est
Dear - est maid - en! Dear - est
Lu - cas! Love to faithful love re - spon-sive Is the
maid - en! Love to faithful love re - spon-sive Is the
p
f
p

high - est pitch of rapture
Heav'n be - stows, be -
high - est pitch of rapture
Heav'n be - stows, be -
f
p
ten.
- stows, Heav'n be - stows . . . . on mor - -
- stows, Heav'n be - stows . . . . on mor - -
f
p
pp
- - - - - - - tal life, on mortal life, . . on mortal
- - - - - - - tal life, on mortal life, . on mortal
cres
life, ... on mortal life. . .
life, ... on mortal life. . .
f
3
f

***No.* 28.** RECIT.—LO! WHERE THE PLENTEOUS HARVEST WAV'D.

No. 29. AIR.—"BEHOLD, ALONG THE DEWY GRASS."

- bedient to command, At - tentive seeks the la-tent prey, At - ten - - tive seeks the
la - tent prey. In search of scent the spaniel roves A -
- long, a-long the dewy grass; And still o - be-dient to command, Attentive seeks the
la -
- - - - - tent, seeks the la - - - tent prey.
Più moto. ♩ = 132.
Più moto.

But press'd by ardour, now he runs, But press'd by ardour, now he runs,
Nor heeds the call, and chid - - ing voice, Nor
heeds the call, and chid - - ing voice,
più moto. ♩ = 160.
Then
più moto.
scent - ing, Then scent - ing the game,
He
sud - den stops, . . . And stiff, with o - pen nose, he stands. . . . .
f
p
p

Th'impending pe-ril to a-
-void, The startled fowl flies instant up; But wings in vain his
ra - - - - pid flight: The gun darts forth,
darts forth its fa-tal charge, And strikes him
dead From the tow'r - - ing height.
f
p
pp
ff

Th' impending pe-ril to a - void, The startled fowl flies instant up; But
wings in vain his ra - - - - pid flight: The
p
gun darts forth its fa - - tal charge, and strikes him
sempre pp
pp
dead From the tow'r - ing height, And strikes him
dead From the tow'r - ing height.
f
3
f

No. 30. RECIT.—"ERE YET THE ORIENT SUN."

The Manuden Singers & Players
Directed by Ian Priest
Present

Josef Haydn

The Seasons

~Autumn & Winter~

Sunday 11th December 2011
at 7.30 pm
St Mary's Church, Manuden

All proceeds to finalising the Church Building Project and Organ Restoration funds

Programme

G F Handel: Concerto Grosso Opus 3 No 2 in B flat

~~~~~

Josef Haydn: Autumn

~~~~~

~~~ Interval ~~~

~~~~~~

G F Handel: Concerto Grosso Opus 3 No 4 in F Major

~~~~~~

Josef Haydn: Winter

~~~~~~

Programme Notes

Handel Concerti Grossi Opus 3: Unlike the twelve concertos of Handel's Opus 6, which are basically string concertos, the six concertos of Opus 3 might almost be considered Handel's answer to Bach's Brandenburg Concertos and his Orchestral Suites, at least in terms of the variety of instrumentation and style of the various movements. In addition to the usual Allegros and Andantes, we find Minuets, Gavottes and grand French style Ouvertures. Instrumentation includes oboes as well as strings. We owe this splendid set of concertos to the enterprise of one John Walsh, an English publisher who clearly saw Handel as a prime source of material. Walsh appears to have persuaded Handel to supply compositions for publication on a regular basis, and in 1734, Handel quickly assembled a collection of six concerti grossi, incorporating favourite music from his previous operas, anthems and sacred works along with new material. As always, Handel can be relied upon to provide cheerful, inventive and appealing fare for players and audience alike in this set.

Haydn: Autumn and Winter from The Seasons: Haydn wrote *The Seasons* following the great success of his previous oratorio The Creation (1798), which had become very popular all over Europe. The libretto for *The Seasons* was provided to Haydn, just as with *The Creation*, by Baron Gottfried van Swieten, an Austrian nobleman who had also exercised an important influence on the career of Mozart. Van Swieten's libretto was his own German translation of extracts from the long English poem "The Seasons" by James Thomson (1700–1748), which had been published in 1730. The composition process was arduous for Haydn, in part because his health was gradually failing and partly because Haydn found van Swieten's libretto to be rather taxing; he took two years to complete the work. The premiere, in Vienna on April 24, 1801, was considered a clear success, but not one comparable to that of *The Creation*. Like *Creation*, *The Seasons* is a bilingual work, and is in effect a secular Oratorio complete with Recitative, Arias and Choruses. Since Haydn was very popular in England (particularly
~~~~~~

following his visits there in 1791–1792 and 1794–1795), he wished the work to be performable in English as well as German. Van Swieten therefore retranslated the Thomson original back into English, fitting it to the rhythm of the music. The resulting English text has not always proven satisfying to listeners and may explain why *Seasons* is less widely performed than *Creation.* But Haydn's music is as always full of delightful inventiveness and charm, as the following notes may help to elucidate.

Autumn

After an introductory overture and recitative, Simon (Bass), Jane (Soprano) and Lucas (Tenor) representing archetypal country folk, together with the likewise bucolic Chorus, sing an ode to **'Toil'**, from which comes every good. Haydn himself had a somewhat quizzical attitude to this libretto, writing that while he had been industrious his whole life long, this was the first occasion he had ever been asked to write a chorus in praise of industry. Nevertheless it is a fine composition and he succumbs to the invitation to provide a good, taxing fugue for the chorus. There follows a charming love **Duet** between Lucas and Jane, relating the fruitfulness of the season to the delights of the honest love they share. In the **Aria** which follows, Simon goes out hunting with his dog, whom Haydn delightfully depicts sniffing the trail of his prey, then speeding up as he approaches it, then pausing before the birds all fly up in alarm at the sound of a shot. Lucas next describes the hares as the Orchestra depicts them scattering in all directions before the approaching **Hunting Chorus**, surely one of the most dramatic depictions of this favourite autumn pastime in all music, and a *tour de force* for the horn section of the orchestra. Haydn's music vividly conveys the thrill of the chase, the bafflement of the hounds when they lose the scent, and the triumph of the denouement. Bringing ***Autumn*** to a fitting close is a wonderful, wine-swilling, thigh-slapping Austrian party, complete with droning bagpipes and screeching fiddles; as the chorus progresses the music become increasingly drunken – and all the more challenging to perform sober!

Winter

The Orchestra introduces this movement with a vivid depiction of the fogs of early winter, followed by Recits from all three soloists describing the characteristically depressing seasonal gloom, cold, damp and desolation of the winter landscape. In the **Aria** which follows, Lucas tells the tale of the winter traveller who struggles to find his path amid the drifting snow until mirage-like, he sees a light ahead denoting the warmth and welcome around the blazing fire of home. In the recits and Arias that follow we are brought inside to share the indoor domestic activity. In the first of two **Songs with Chorus** Jane leads the womenfolk in spinning flax, a chorus which Haydn casts in the minor key, hinting at the somewhat sinister connotations that always seem to attach to the spinning wheel in folklore. The second **Song with Chorus** is much more cheerful, with Jane telling the story of the pretty maid who outwits the advances of the country squire, to the general approval of the listeners gathered round. Simon then takes the following **Recit and Aria** to review the passing of the Seasons, regretting the disappearance of the times of plenty and the nights of revelry, leaving only Virtue behind. Before drawing to a close, the **Chorus** looks forward longingly to the still distant Spring (in fact, we have somewhat artificially borrowed this Chorus from the opening *Spring* section of the Oratorio, just to cheer ourselves up). Finally Soloists and Chorus join together in a movement which at last brings us, by way of another bracing fugue, 'into the glorious realm of Heaven'.

The Soloists

Amy Worsfold, Soprano; Jeff Phillips, Tenor; James Priest, Bass

The Manuden Singers

Soprano: Tricia Barber, Valerie Bartram, Fiona Bengtsen, Hilary Green, Philippa Harris, Rosemary Harrison, Carol Hunt, Pat Larby, Hilly Mills, Daphne Morton, Anne Spence, Shirley Gooch, Lisa Walker, Janie Watson

Alto: Jenny Clack, Annette Farrimond, Sue Griffiths, Teresa Priest, Leila Ridell, Barbara Weatherup, Carol Wylde, Jane Woodhouse.

Tenor: Rob Clack, Richard Lewin, Huw Lewis, Anthony Ratcliffe, Fran Richards, David Sheppard, Daniel Woods

Bass: Sean Brady, David Green, Alan Lumsden, Bill O'Neil, Richard Prince, Dick Prime,

The Manuden Players

Violin 1: Ysobel Latham (Leader), Govan Bramley, Simon Jackson, Miriam Henson

Violin 2: Philippa Brown, Marion Stringer, Mary Williams

Viola: Leslie Dimsdale, Jonathan Ecclestone, Patrick Hamilton,

Cello: David Plowman, Isabella Warren, John Wigley

Bass: Tim Stone

Flute: Clare Griffiths, Janine Parker

Oboes: Gerald Stainer, Jane Cursiter

Clarinet: Andrew Pummell, Jo Wood

Bassoon: Judy Corkhill,

Trumpet: Toby & Georgia Bruce-Jones

Horns: Christina de Jong Clyndert, Philippa Scott

Timpani: Robin Osterley

Continuo: Richard Latham

~~~~~~
~~~~~~

Amy Worsfold, Soprano: A native of Surrey, Amy is delighted to be singing for the first time in Manuden. A graduate of York University, and now studying with Jenevora Williams, her career has seen her so far singing with small companies around London and churches near her home town in Surrey, as well as concerts further afield around England. Opera is her forte, with notable recent appearances as Emmie (for Surrey Opera), in the world premiere of Chance: A Street Opera for the Tete a Tete Opera Festival, and various ladies in the operas of Mozart, Britten... And the odd bit of Gilbert and Sullivan!

Jeff Phillips, Tenor: Jeff Phillips has sung with a variety of semi-professional and amateur groups, including the BBC Welsh Chorus, the Chelsea Opera Group, the National Eisteddfod Choir and various university choirs and opera groups, in a wide variety of choral music, and operas ranging from Handel to Richard Strauss via Verdi, Puccini and some Frenchmen. Musical career highlight = propping up the bar with Max Boyce: Low point = singing Dvořák in Welsh.

James Priest, Bass: Beginning his singing career at Bishops Stortford College, James went on to study music at Birmingham University in parallel with voice and piano at the Birmingham Conservatoire, and then to study for a Masters in Performance in Voice at Trinity College of Music in London where he won a scholarship. He has developed a wide range of operatic and oratorio roles, and was a prize winner in the 2011 Essex Young Musician Competition. Career highlights to date have included a year's apprenticeship with the Monteverdi Choir under Sir John Eliot Gardiner (granted to only eight young musicians in the UK) which featured Prom Concert performances and tours in Europe. Recent and upcoming solo engagements include Christmas Oratorio in Truro Cathedral, Butterworth's Shropshire Lad with the Uttlesforde Orchestra in February and Beethoven's Mass in C at St Pauls Knightsbridge in March.

The Manuden Players are all accomplished instrumentalists from around the district, who have given freely of their time and talents to support our concert. Handel and Haydn can be relied upon to provide joyous and festive fare for the enjoyment of players and audience alike. We thank the Players warmly for joining us this evening.

Forthcoming Concert

As part of the Celebrations of the Diamond Jubilee of Her Majesty the Queen, The Manuden Singers & Players will present a

Jubilee Promenade Concert

In St Mary's Church, Manuden on Sunday 15 April 2012 at 7.30 pm

~~~~~

If you have enjoyed this Concert and would like details of our further performances please email us on itp@dsl.pipex.com; better still, encourage your friends to do so as well.
~~~~~

Vivace. ♩. = 112.
. . light-ed throng.
Vivace. Corni.
No. 31 Chorus.—HARK! THE MOUNTAINS RESOUND.
f Tutti. Tenor.
Hark! . . Hark! the mountains re - sound! . . The vales and fo-rests
f Tutti. Bass.
Hark! . . Hark! the mountains re- sound! Hark! the mountains re- sound! The
ring! . . The vales and fo-rests ring! . . . . .
vales and fo- rests ring, ...
Viol.
Corni.
Soprano.
f Tutti.
Hark!
Alto.
Tutti.
Hark! the moun - tains,
Tenor.
Bass.

hark, the mountains re-sound, . . . The vales and fo - rests ring!
hark, the mountains resound, The vales and fo - rests ring!
fz
fz
Corni.
f
It is . . . the shril - - ly sound - ing
It is . . . the shril - - ly sound - ing
It is . . . the shril - - ly sound - . ing
It is . . . the shril - - ly sound - ing
horn! The cry of the hounds and the
horn! The cry of the hounds and the
horn! The cry of the hounds and the
horn! The cry of the hounds and the
fz
fz

huntsman, the hounds and the hunts - man!
huntsman, the hounds and the hunts - man!
huntsman, the hounds and the hunts - man!
huntsman, the hounds and the hunts - man!
Corni.
A
The stag, . . . by fear a - rous'd, is
The stag, by fear a - rous'd, is
A
up,
And ea-ger, and ea-ger men, horses and dogs pur- sue.
up,
And ea-ger, and ea- ger men, horses, and dogs pur- sue.
Corni.

K

He flies. he flies!
He flies, he flies!
He flies!
He flies!
Ob.
Viol.
Behold how he bounds!
Behold how he bounds!
Behold how he bounds!
Behold how he bounds!
8ves.
loco.
And ea-ger, and ea-ger men, horses, and dogs pur - sue. . .
And ea-ger, and ea-ger men, horses, and dogs pur - sue. . .
And ea-ger, and ea-ger men, horses, and dogs pur - sue. . .
And ea-ger, and ea-ger men, horses, and dogs pur - sue. . .
fz

His ra - pid flight,
His ra - pid flight,
His ra - pid flight,
His ra - pid flight,
fz
fz
His ra - pid flight out-strips the wind.
His ra - pid flight out-strips the wind.
His ra - pid flight out-strips the wind.
His ra - pid flight out-strips the wind.
B
Thro'
Thro'
Thro'
Corni.
Viol.
B
f

copse and thicket be - hold . . how he bursts! And skims . . o'er the
copse and thicket be - hold how he bursts! And skims o'er the
copse and thicket be - hold . . how he bursts! And skims . o'er the
plains, . . to the shel - - tering wood.
plains, . . to the shel - - tering wood.
plains, . . to the shel - - tering wood.
ff
Corni.
1st Tenor.
And doubt - - ful
2nd Tenor.
The pack are now at fault,
And doubt - - ful
Bass.
The pack are now at fault,
And doubt - - ful

C Soprano.
They stray dispers'd a - round, . . .
Alto.
where to bend their course,
They stray dispers'd a - round, . . .
Tenor.
where to bend their course.
They stray dispers'd a - round, . . .
Bass.
where to bend their course.
They stray dispers'd a - round, . . .
C
fz
fz
fz
They stray . . . dis - pers'd . . . a - round,
They stray . . . dis - pers'd . . . a - round,
They stray . . . dis - pers'd . . . a - round,
They stray . . . dis - pers'd . . . a - round,
f
fz
fz
Tally ho!
Tally ho!
Tally ho! . Tally ho! . . . Tally ho!
Tally ho! . Tally ho! . . . Tally ho!
3
3

The huntsman's voice and sound - ing horn Have brought . . them
The huntsman's voice and sound - ing horn Have brought . . them
Ho! ho! ho! . . Tal-ly
Ho! ho! ho! . . Tal-ly
back a-gain. Ho! . . ho! ho! ho! . . Tal-ly ho! . . Tal-ly
back a-gain. Ho! . . ho! ho! ho . . Tal-ly ho! . . Tal-ly
ff
ho! ho! ho!
ho! ho! ho!
ho! ho! ho!
ho! ho! ho!

D
With ar-dour e - lat - - ed, Rash - - ly pours . a -
With ar-dour e - lat - ed, Rash - ly, rash - ly pours a -
With ar-dour e - lat - ed, Rash - ly, rash - ly pours a -
With ar-dour e - lat - ed, Rash - ly
D
fz
fz
fz
- - long, ... O'er the plains . . the re - joic - - ing
- long, O'er the plains . . the re - joic - - - - - - - ing
- long, O'er the plains . . . . the re - j 'c - - ing
pours a-long, O'er the plains . . . . the re - joic - - ing
throng.
throng.
throng. Tally ho! . . Tally ho! . . Tally
throng. Tally ho! . . Tally ho! . . Tally

SOPRANO.
ho!
Sur-rounded now on ev - 'ry side, His spi-rits and his
ALTO.
ho!
Sur-round-ed now on ev - 'ry side, His spi-rits and his
vi-gour lost, Ex - haust - ed drops . . the trem-bling deer.
vi-gour lost, Ex - haust - ed drops . . the trem-bling deer.
E
TENOR.
A-gain the mer-ry horn re-sounds,
BASS.
A-gain the mer-ry horn re-sounds,
A-gain the mer-ry horn re-sounds, And cla - morous shout . . the
A-gain the mer-ry horn re-sounds, And cla - morous shout . . the
Ped.

joy - ous crowds, Hur-rah! . . . . Hur-
joy - ous crowds, Hur-rah! . . . . Hur-
- - rah! . . Hur-rah! . . . . A-gain the merry horn resounds,
SOPRANO.
ALTO.
- - rah! . . Hur-rah! . . . . A-gain the merry horn resounds,
fz
A-gain the mer-ry horn re - sounds, And cla - - morous
A-gain the mer-ry horn re - sounds, And cla - - morous
fz
shout . . the joy - ous crowds. Hur - rah! . . .
F
shout . . the joy - ous crowds. Hur - rah! . . .
TENOR.
Hur - rah! . .
BASS.
A - gain the mer - ry
fz fz ff fz

Hur - rah! . . And cla - - morous
Hur - rah! . . . . . And cla - - morous
Hur - rah! . . . And cla - - morous
horn resounds, A - gain the mer - ry horn resounds, And cla - - - morous
fz
fz
shout . . the joy - ous crowds, Hur -
shout . . the joy - ous crowds, Hur -
shout . . the joy - - ous crowds, Hur -
shout . . the joy - - ous crowds, A -
- rah! . . . Hur - rah! . . . And cla - - morous
- rah! . . . Hur - rah! . . . And cla - - mo-rous
- rah! . . . Hur - rah! . . . And cla - - mo-rous
- gain the mer-ry horn resounds, A - gain the mer-ry horn resounds, And cla - - - mo-rous
fz

G
shout . . . the joy - ous crowds.
shout . . . the joy - ous crowds.
shout . . . the joy - - ous crowds. Hur-rah! . . . .
shout . . . the joy - - ous crowds. Hur-rah!
G
Hur-rah! . . Hur-rah! . . . .
Hur-rah! . . Hur-rah! . . . .
Hur -
Hur-rah! . . .
fz
ff
8ves.
Hur-rah! . . . .
Hur-rah! . . . .
- rah! . . Hur-rah! . . . .
. . . Hur-rah! . . . .
Ped.
ff
Ped.
8ves.

No. 82. RECIT.—"THE VINEYARD NOW ITS WEALTH DISPLAYS."

No. 33.
CHORUS.—JOYFUL THE LIQUOR FLOWS.
Allegro molto.
TREBLE.
ALTO.
TENOR (8ve. lower).
BASS.
ACCOMP.
♩= 166.
Joy - - ful, joy - - ful the li - quor flows, The bul - ky tuns are fill'd; Let plea - sure reign a - round, And joy, . . and
Joy - - ful, joy - - ful the li - quor flows, The bul - ky tuns are fill'd; Let plea - sure reign a-round, And joy, . . and
Joy - - ful, joy - - ful the li - quor flows, The bul - ky tuns are fill'd; Let plea-sure reign a-round, And joy, . . and
Joy - - ful, joy - - ful the li - quor flows, The bul - ky tuns are fill'd; Let plea-sure reign a-round, And joy, . . and

fz
joy in loud-est strains re - sound! Let plea - - sure
joy in loud-est strains re - sound! Let plea - - sure
joy in loud-est strains re - sound! Let plea - - sure
joy in loud-est strains re- sound! Let plea - - sure
reign a-round, And joy, . . and joy in loud-est strains re -
reign a-round, And joy, and joy in loud-est strains re -
reign a-round, And joy, . . and joy in loud-est strains re -
reign a-round, And joy, . . and joy in loud-est strains re -
fz
A
-sound.
-sound.
-sound. Free from sor - row, let us re - vel, Fill'd with
-sound. Free from sor - row, let us re - vel, Fill'd with
p

In glad cho - rus raise your
In glad cho - rus raise your
mirth and glee.
mirth and glee.
fz
voices, Merry, mer - ry be. Joy! joy! joy! All hail to the
voices, Merry, mer - ry be, Joy! joy! joy! All hail to the
Joy! joy! joy! All hail to the
Joy! joy! All hail to the
fz
f
B
wine! Joy - ful sing! All
wine! Joy - ful sing! All
wine! And hail to the land that brings it forth! Joy - ful sing! All
wine! And hail to the land that brings it forth! Joy-ful sing! All
p
f

fz
hail to the wine! Joy - ful sing! All
fz
hail to the wine! Joy - ful sing! All
fz
hail to the wine! The ves-sel be prais'd that gives it strength! Joy-ful sing! All
fz
hail to the wine! The ves-sel be prais'd that gives it strength! Joy-ful sing! All
p
f
fz
hail to the wine! Joy - ful sing! All
fz
hail to the wine! Joy - ful sing! All
fz
hail to the wine! And prais'd be the bowl from whence it flows! Joy - ful sing! All
fz
hail to the wine! And prais'd be the bowl from whence it flows! Joy - ful sing! All
p
cres.
f
hail to the wine! Joy - ful sing! All hail to the wine! Sing, oh,
hail to the wine! Joy - ful sing! All hail to the wine! Sing, oh,
hail to the wine! Joy - ful, joy - ful sing! Joy- ful, joy - ful sing! All
hail to the wine! Joy - ful, joy - ful sing! Joy - ful, joy - ful sing! All
fz
fz
fz
fz

C

. . sing! All hail to the wine! All hail to the wine!

. . sing! All hail to the wine! All hail to the wine!

hail to the wine! All hail, all hail to the wine!

hail to the wine! All hail, all hail to the wine!

fz Ped. *

Come, com - pa-nions, fill the tankard, Drain the gob-let; jo-cund let us be!

Come, com - pa-nions, fill the tankard, Drain the gob-let; jo - cund let us be!

Drain the gob-let; jo - cund let us be! And hail to the

jo-cund, jo - cund let us be! And hail to the

jo-cund, jo - cund let us be! And hail to the

jo-cund, jo - cund let us be! And hail to the

fz

fz
wine! in loud-est strains re-sound; Joy - - ful, joy-
wine! in loud-est strains re-sound; Oh sing, oh
wine! in loud-est strains re-sound; Joy - - ful, oh
wine! in loud-est strains re-sound; Oh sing, oh
sf
fz
- - ful, All hail to the wine!
sing, oh sing, All hail to the wine!
sing, All hail to the wine!
sing, oh sing, All hail to the wine!
D
♩. = 88.
Allegro assai.
mezzo.
p
pp
Soprano.
The mer-ry-toned fife and the drum are re-sounding, The fife and the
Alto.
The mer-ry-toned fife and the drum are re-sounding, The fife and the
f

drum are resounding,
The drums are re-sound-ing,
drum are re-sounding,
The drums are re-sound-ing,
p
ff
The bag-pipe prolongs the hum . . . . . of its drone,
The bag-pipe prolongs the hum . . . of its drone,
fz
fz
The hum of its drone, ... the hum, the hum of its drone,
The hum of its drone, ... the hum, the hum of its drone,
fz
p
fz
fz
fz
E
Tenor.
While sporting and dancing,
While
Bass.
While sporting and dancing,
While
E

sport-ing and dancing The nymphs are ad-vanc-ing,
All
sport-ing and dancing The nymphs are ad-vanc-ing,
All
mirthful and joy-ous, what pas-time they're courting!
With fro-lic and glee,
mirthful and joy-ous, what pastime they're courting!
With fro-lic and glee,
Treble.
Trip it, trip it, quick and sprightly.
Alto.
Trip it, trip it, quick and sprightly.
fz
Tenor.
Trip it, trip it, quick and spright-ly.
Com-pa-nions, come!
Bass.
Trip it, trip it, quick and spright-ly.
Com-pa-nions, come!
fz
fz

SOPRANO.
Trip it, trip it, Quick and sprightly,
TENOR.
The tankards
ALTO.
Trip it, trip it, Quick and sprightly,
BASS.
The tankards
fill, the tankards fill!
F
SOPRANO.
Trip it, trip it, Quick and sprightly,
fill, the tankards fill!
ALTO.
Trip it, trip it, Quick and sprightly,
ff
F
TENOR.
The gob - lets drain! The gob - lets drain!
BASS.
The gob - lets drain! The gob - lets drain!
SOPRANO.
Jo - cund, jo - cund, jo - cund let us be, jo - cund, jo - cund
ALTO.
Jo - cund, jo - cund let us be, jo-cund, jo - cund let us
TENOR.
Jo - cund, jo - cund, jo-cund let . . . .
BASS.
Jo - cund, jo - cund let us be, jo - cund, jo - cund

let us be. Hail! all hail . . to the wine! In loud - est strains re -
let us be. Hail! all hail to the wine! In loud - est strains re -
. . us be Hail! all hail . . to the wine! In loud - est strains re -
let us be. Hail! all hail to the wine! In loud - est strains re -
fz
G
-sound.
-sound.
-sound. Re - vel, ri - - ot! Re - vel,
-sound. Re - - vel, ri - - ot!
fz
G
fz
fz
fz
fz
fz
Hail! all hail to the wine! to the wine all hail!
Hail! . . to the wine! to the
re - vel, ri - ot! Re -
fz
fz
fz
fz
fz

All hail to . . the wine!
wine! to the
- - - vel, re - vel, ri - - - ot!
re - vel, ri - ot!
fz fz fz fz fz
Cheer-ly, cheer - ly trip!
wine! Cheer-ly, cheer - ly trip!
Frisk and gam-bol, laugh and ca - rol, re - vel,
Frisk and gam-bol, laugh and ca - rol,
fz fz fz fz fz
Cheer - ly, cheer - ly, cheer-ly trip,
Cheer-ly, cheer-ly trip,
ri - ot,
re - vel, ri - ot,
fz fz fz fz

Mer - ri-ly, merri - ly, brisk - ly trip! Push . . it on, Press it on,
Mer-ri - ly, mer-ri-ly, brisk - ly trip! Push it on, Press it on,
Now let us brim the foam-ing cup,
Now let us brim the foam- ing cup, now
Send it a-round! Push it on, Press it on, Send it a-
Send it a-round! Push . . it on, Press it on,
Now let us brim the foam - ing cup,
let us brim the foam -ing cup,
fz
-round! Then let us sing, Then let us sing in
Send it a - round! Then let us sing, then let us sing in
Then let us sing in cho - rus full, The joy - ous pro-duce
Then let us sing in cho - rus full, The joy - ous pro - duce from the

cho - rus full, The joy - ous pro - duce from the grape, Push it on,
cho - rus full, The joy - ous pro - duce from the grape, Push . . it
from the grape, from the grape, from the grape, Push . . it
grape, Press . . it on, Send it, send it a-round, Push . . it on, Send it
fz
fz
fz
Press it on, Send it, send it a - round! All hail to the wine, Old
on, Push it on, on! All hail to the wine, Old
on, Push it on, on! All hail to the wine, Old
send it a-round, Push it on, on! All hail to the wine, Old
ff
H
age - 's friend, Of care and grief the cure! With voice of loud re -
age - 's friend, Of care and grief the cure! With voice of loud re -
age - 's friend, Of care and grief the cure! With voice of loud re -
age - 's friend, Of care and grief the cure! With voice of loud re -

-sound-ing mirth, The gen' - rous li - quor let us praise, the gen' - rous li - quor
-sound-ing mirth, The gen' - rous li - quor let us praise,
-sound-ing mirth, The gen' - rous li - quor let us praise,
-sound-ing mirth, The gen' - rous li - quor let us praise, the gen' - rous li - quor
let us praise, Let us praise with voice of mirth, let us praise with
Let . . . us praise . . with voice of mirth, let us praise with
Let . . . us praise . . with voice of mirth, let us praise with
let us praise, Let us praise with
voice of mirth, with voice . . of loud resound-ing mirth, resound-ing mirth, the
voice of mirth, with voice . . of loud resound-ing mirth, resound-ing mirth, the
voice of mirth, with voice . . of loud resound-ing mirth, resound-ing mirth, the
voice of mirth, with voice . . of loud resound-ing mirth, resound-ing mirth, the
fz
fz

END OF AUTUMN.

WINTER.

No. 34. INTRODUCTION.

Expressing the thick fogs at the approach of WINTER.

Adagio ma non troppo.

PIANO.

♩ = 60.

p *f* *fz* *p* *sempre legato.* *fz* *fz* *f* *fz* *p* *p* tr

No. 35. RECIT.—NOW SINKS THE PALE DECLINING YEAR.

No. 36. CAVATINA.—"LIGHT AND LIFE DEJECTED LANGUISH."

No 37. RECIT.—"A CRYSTAL PAVEMENT LIES THE LAKE"

No. 38. Air. — THE TRAV'LER STANDS PERPLEX'D.
Presto. ♩= 166.
Lucas.
Piano.
Presto. f
p
sempre p
sempre staccato.
sempre staccato.
f
The trav'-ler stands per-plex'd, For-lorn, un-cer-tain he, Which way his wan-d'ring, wand'ring steps to turn, to turn A-cross the trackless waste.
No hu-man dwell-ing cheers his sight, No mark of human foot is found, No mark of human foot is found;
No human dwelling cheers his sight, No mark, no mark of foot. . . is found.

No mark of human foot is found; And
onward as he bravely toils, In deeper er-ror plun-ges still, In deeper er-ror plunges still, In
sempre staccato.
deep - er er - - - ror plun - ges still. De-
f
p
- press'd his cou - rage sinks, And an - guish wrings his heart, As
pp
night its sa - ble horrors sheds, And wea - ri - ness and cold Have
pp
stiff - - en'd all . . . . his limbs. De-press'd his cou - rage

sinks, And an - guish wrings his heart! Before his glad - den'd
sight ap - pears A sud - den gleam of neighb'ring light;
Allegro. ♩ = 144.
And now reviv'd he springs,
With joyful panting breast, with joyful panting breast,
To gain the door, To gain the welcome, welcome door,
Where all his pains may find . . re - lief! And

now, re-viv'd, he springs With joy - - - - - - -
p
f
- ful, with joy ful panting breast, with joy-ful panting breast, To
pp
p
gain the door, to gain the welcome, welcome door, To gain . . .
the welcome door, Where
pp
all his pains may find . . . re - lief, may . . find re - lief, may . .
find . . . re-lief.
f
p
f
fz
fz

No. 39. RECIT.—"AS HE DRAWS NIGH."

No. 40. CHORUS.—"LET THE WHEEL MOVE GAILY."

Twist - ing fine and ten - der threads, Vir - gin cheeks to shel - ter.
f
A CHORUS.
Let the wheel move gai - - - ly, Sing - ing as it cir - cles,
CHORUS.
Let the wheel move gai - - - ly, Sing - ing as it cir - cles,
A
fz
fz
p
JANE.
Gen - tle wea-ver, make thy web Clear and fine, of dex - 'trous art,
Gracing her that wears it.
Gen-tle weaver,
p
make thy web Clear and fine, of dex-t'rous art, Grac - ing her that
fz

B
CHORUS.
wears it. Let the wheel move gai - ly, Sing - ing as it
CHORUS.
Let the wheel move gai - ly, Sing - ing as it
B
fz
fz
f
JANE.
cir - - cles. Pure with-in as fair with-out, Ought the vir - gin
cir - - cles.
p
breast to be, Loveliest in con - ceal - ment,
p
Pure with-in as fair without, Ought the vir - gin breast to be,
C CHORUS.
Loveli - est in con - ceal-ment. Let the wheel move gai - ly,
CHORUS.
Let the wheel move gai - ly,
C
f
fz
fz
fz

JANE.
Sing - ing as it cir - cles. Pure with-in as fair without,
Sing - ing as it cir - cles.
p
Mo - dest, gen-tle, heed - ful minds, Best se-cure af - fec - tion.
TREBLE.
D
CHORUS.
Pure with-in as fair with-out,
ALTO.
CHORUS.
Pure with-in as fair with-out,
TENOR.
CHORUS.
Pure with-in as fair with-out,
BASS.
CHORUS.
Pure with-in as fair with-out,
D
f
fz
Mo-dest, gen-tle, heed-ful minds, Best se-cure af - fec - tion;
Mo-dest, gen - tle, heed - ful minds, Best secure af - fec - tion;
Mo-dest, gen-tle, heed - ful minds, Best se-cure af - fec - tion;
Mo-dest, gen- tle, heed - ful minds, Best se-cure af - fec - tion;
fz

Pure with-in as fair without, Mo - dest, gen-tle,
Pure with-in as fair without, Mo - dest, gen-tle,
Pure with-in as fair without, Mo - dest, gen-tle,
Pure with-in as fair with-out, Mo - dest, gen-tle,
heed-ful minds, Best se-cure af-fec - tion, Best . . . se-
heed-ful minds, Best se-cure af-fec - tion, Best . . se-
heed-ful minds, Best se-cure af-fec - tion, Best . . . se-
heed-ful minds, Best se-cure af-fec - tion, Best . . se-
-cure . . af-fec - - - - - tion.
-cure . . af-fec - - - - - tion.
-cure . . af-fec - - - - - tion.
-cure . . af-fec - - - - - tion.
ten.
fz
fz
dim.
p
pp

No. 41. RECIT.—"THE EV'NING'S TASK ANON PERFORM'D."
LUCAS.
The ev'ning's task anon perform'd, Col-lect-ed now they sit Around the sparkling fire, With eager
looks and ears in-tent, To lis - ten to the newest tale, which cheerful Jane has now to tell.
No. 42. AIR AND CHORUS.—"A WEALTHY LORD, WHO LONG HAD LOV'D."
Moderato. ♩=88.
PIANO.
JANE.
A wealthy lord, who long had lov'd An ho - nest coun-try lass, By
chance, with-in a lone - ly vale The gen-tle maid es-pied. Dis -
ten.
fz
pp
f

-mounting from his horse, he said, Come give me one sweet kiss, Come give me one sweet kiss! To
which the frighten'd girl re-plied, O yes with all . . . my heart. Ha, sil-ly girl, why an-swer
A
TREBLE.
ALTO.
Ha, sil-ly girl, why an-swer
TENOR.
Ha, sil - ly, sil - ly
BASS.
Ha, sil - ly, sil - ly
JANE.
so? why not say no? why not say no? Be calm, my pret-ty lass, said he, On
so? why not say no? why not say no?
girl, why answer so? why not say no? why not say no?
girl, why answer so? why not say no? why not say no?
me bes-tow thy heart. For true and constant is my love, Not i-dle trifling sport,

Thou shalt be hap-py! Take this purse, this watch and glitt'-ring
p
ring. And ask whate'er thy heart can wish, Thou shalt not want it
B
CHORUS.
long. In-deed, In-deed, that's shrewdly urg'd, that's shrewdly urg'd, that's shrewdly urg'd, No,
JANE.
CHORUS.
In-deed, indeed, that's shrewdly urg'd, that's shrewdly urg'd that's shrewdly urg'd.
CHORUS.
In-deed, in-deed, in - deed, that's shrewdly urg'd, indeed, indeed, that's shrewdly urg'd.
CHORUS.
In-deed, in-deed, in - deed, that's shrewdly urg'd, indeed, indeed, that's shrewdly urg'd.
B
f
no, she cried, I must not leave My sim-ple hap-py home, My brother toiling for my sake, My
p

fa-ther full of love. In yonder field, the plough he guides, Per-
pp
f
p
pp
- haps — if they—but, no. Be - yond the hedge quite close at hand, Be-
f
p
pp
f
C
CHORUS.
JANE.
- hold them at their toil. Ha, ha! what next, I pray, what next, I pray, what next, I pray? And
CHORUS.
Ha, ha! what next, I pray, what next, I pray, what next, I pray?
CHORUS.
Ha, ha! ha, ha! what next, I pray, what next, I pray, what next, I pray?
CHORUS.
Ha, ha! ha, ha! what next, I pray, what next, I pray, what next, I pray?
C
f
fz
now, as o'er the hedge he peeps, The maid, with sudden spring, Leaps up up-on his horse, and swift Its
p

master leaves behind,
Fare - well, she cries, my gen'rous lord! My
wrongs I thus re - venge.
Asham'd and vex'd he ga-ping stands, To
see her thus escape.
D
CHORUS.
Ha, ha, ha, ha, in truth well done, in truth well done, ha, ha, ha, ha, in truth well done, ha, ha, ha,
ha, in truth well done, ha, ha, ha, ha, in truth well done, in truth well done, in truth well
Ha, ha, in truth well done, in truth well done, ha, ha, ha, ha,
in truth well done, ha, ha, in truth . . well done, in truth well done, in truth well
ha, in truth well done, ha, ha, ha, ha, in truth well done, in truth well done, in truth well
ha, ha, in truth well done, ha, ha, ha, ha, in truth . . well done, in truth well done, in truth well
Ha, ha, in truth well done, in truth well done, ha, ha, ha, ha,
in truth well done, ha, ha, in truth well done, ha, ha, ha, ha, in truth well done, ha, ha, ha, ha, in truth well

done, ha, ha, ha, ha, in truth, well done, ha, ha, ha, ha, in truth well done, in truth well done.
done, ha, ha, ha, ha, in truth, . . well done, ha, ha, ha, ha, in truth well done, in truth well done.
done, ha, ha, ha, ha, in truth . . well done, ha, ha, ha, ha, in truth well done, in truth well done.
done, in truth well done, ha, ha, ha, ha, in truth well done, in truth well done.
fz
ff
ff
No. 43.
RECIT.—" FROM OUT THE EAST."
SIMON.
From out the east there darts an i - cy gale, Whose piercing cold, fierce spreading thro' the
p
sky, All damp and mist as-sails and e'en the breath of li-ving things. The tyrant influence reigns from pole to
pole, And na-ture lies a vast ex - ten - ded waste In-wrapt in si - lent gloom.
p

No. 44. AIR.—" IN THIS, O VAIN MISGUIDED MAN

fz
Win - - - - ter last, with drea - ry close, Meet
em - - - - blem of the yawn - - - ing tomb, And
Win - - - - - ter last with drea - ry close, Meet
em - - - - blem of the yawn - - - - ing tomb;
ten.
ten.
p
p
Allegro molto. 𝅗𝅥 = 92.
Where now are fled thy lof - ty
Allegro molto.
f
p

schemes,
Thy flat - t'ring hopes of
f
3
wealth,
Thy long - ings af - ter
3
fame,
And all thy world - ly cares?
f
p
fz
Where now are fled the mirth-ful days,
fz
fz
fz
p
pp
In wan - - ton plea - sure past?
Where

now are fled the mirth - - ful days, . . . In
wan - ton plea-sure past? And where, a -
- las! those fes - tive nights, In gid - - - - - - dy
re - vels spent? And where those fes - tive nights, In
gid - dy re - vels spent? Where, where, a - las! where?
f
fz
p
cres.
pp

All va - nish'd, va - nish'd like a dream!

For nought but truth re - mains. . . . . . .

No. 45. RECIT.—TRUTH ONLY LASTS.

No. 46. Trio and Chorus.—"THEN COMES THE DAWN."

Allegro moderato. ♩=104.

SIMON.

Then comes the dawn of that great morn, The Sa - viour's migh - ty voice awakes The dawn of se - cond life, From pain and death for ev - er free; The dawn of second life, From pain and death for ev - er free.

LUCAS.

The heav'n - ly gates are

SIMON.

The heav'n - ly gates are

f *p* *pp*

lift - ed up, The ho - ly hill ap-pears! And on its brow the sacred
lift - ed up, The ho - ly hill ap-pears! And on its brow the sacred
f
p
seat, Where peace e - ter - nal dwells; And on its brow the sacred
seat, Where peace e - ter - nal dwells; And on its brow the sacred
f
p
A
1st Chorus. Tutti.
f
But
Tutti.
f
But
Tutti. f
seat, Where peace e - ter - nal dwells; But
Tutti.
f
seat, Where peace e - ter - nal dwells; But
pp
A
f

JANE.
who shall dare those gates to pass? The man whose life was
who shall dare those gates to pass?
LUCAS.
who shall dare those gates to pass? The man whose life was
SIMON.
who shall dare those gates to pass? The man whose life was
fz
dim.
p
in - cor-rupt.
2nd Chorus. Tutti.
f
And who the ho - ly hill as-cend?
Tutti.
And who the ho - ly hill as-cend?
in - cor-rupt.
Tutti.
And who the ho - ly hill as-cend?
in - cor-rupt.
Tutti.
And who the ho - ly hill as-cend?
JANE.
The man whose tongue . . was void of guile.
B
1st Chorus. Tutti.
What
Tutti.
What
LUCAS.
The man whose tongue . . was void . . of guile.
Tutti.
What
SIMON.
The man whose tongue was void of guile.
Tutti.
What
dim.
p
f

JANE.
soul with - in that seat may dwell? That soul which suc - cours
soul with - in that seat may dwell?
LUCAS.
soul with - in that seat may dwell? That soul which suc - cours
SIMON.
soul with - in that seat may dwell? That soul which suc - cours
p
2ND CHORUS. Tutti.
want and grief. E - ter - nal peace who shall enjoy?
Tutti.
E - ter - nal peace who shall enjoy?
Tutti.
want and grief. E - ter - nal peace who shall enjoy?
Tutti.
want and grief. E - ter - nal peace who shall enjoy?
JANE.
1ST CHORUS. Tutti.
The man who gave the guilt - less aid. The e - - ver-lasting gates of
Tutti.
The e - - verlast-ing gates of
LUCAS.
Tutti.
The man who gave the guilt - less aid. The e - - ver-lasting gates of
SIMON.
Tutti.
The man who gave the guilt - less aid. The e - - ver-lasting gates of

2ND CHORUS.
1ST and 2ND CHORUS.
life, Be-hold! are lift-ed up! The
cres.
f
ff
C
great, the glo-rious morn awakes, The ho-ly hill ap-
1ST CHORUS.
2ND CHORUS.
1ST CHORUS.
-pears! Now are they gone, for e-ver past, The hours of grief and

2ND CHORUS.
1ST and 2ND CHORUS.
pain, . . The storms of mortal life. A calm e - ter - - nal
pain, The storms of mortal life. A calm e - ter - - nal
pain, The storms of mortal life. A calm e - ter - - nal
pain, The storms of mortal life. A calm e - ter - - nal
reigns, And ev - er-last - ing hap - piness Is vir - tue's high re -
reigns, And ev - er-last - ing hap - piness Is vir - tue's high re -
reigns, And ev - er-last - ing hap - piness Is vir - tue's high re -
reigns, And ev - er-last - ing hap - piness Is vir - tue's high re -
ff
JANE.
-ward. May we a like re - ward deserve! May our wishes,
-ward
LUCAS.
-ward. May we a like re - ward deserve! May our wishes,
SIMON.
-ward. May we a like re - ward deserve! May our wishes,
p
p

1st Chorus.
2nd Chorus.
ev'ry ac-tion,
All our labours,
still un-wearied,
All our labours,
still un-wearied,
ev'ry ac-tion,
All our labours,
still un-wearied,
ev'ry ac-tion,
All our labours,
still un-wearied,
1st and 2nd Chorus.
To that glo - ry on - ly tend.
To that glo - ry on - ly tend.
To that glo - ry on - ly tend.
To that glo - ry on - ly tend.
Di-
8ve.
D
Di - rect us in Thy ways, O
- rect us in Thy ways, O God! Support us in the strife! Sup - port . . . . .
D
8ves.

God! Support us in the strife! support us, sup-port . . . . .
Di-rect us in Thy ways, O God! Sup-
. . . . . . us in the strife, in the strife!
fz
f
Di-rect us in Thy ways, O God! Sup-port us in the strife,
. . . us in the strife, in the strife, O God! O God! sup-port us in the strife, Di-
-port us in the strife! sup-port . . . . us in the strife, Di-rect us
Di-rect us in Thy
sup-port us in the strife, support us in the strife!
E
-rect us, di-rect us in . . . Thy ways, O God!
in Thy ways, O God! Sup-port . . . us in the strife, sup-port, ...
ways, O God! Di-rect us in Thy ways, O

Sup-port . . . . us, sup -
Di-rect us in Thy ways, O God! O God! Sup - port . . .
. . . us in the strife! Sup - port . .
God! O God! Sup -
- port . . . . us, sup - port . . . . us in the
. . us, sup - port . . . . us, O God! in the strife, O God!
. . . us, sup - port . . . . us in the
- port . . . . us, sup-port us, sup-port us in the strife, in the
strife, sup - port . . . . . us, support us, support us in the
sup - port . . . us in the strife, sup-port us, sup - port us in the strife, in the
strife, sup - port us, sup - port us, sup -
strife, sup - port . . . us in the strife, sup-port us, sup - port us, support us in the

strife!
Di-rect us in Thy ways, O God! Sup-
strife, sup-port... us in the strife! Di-rect us in Thy ways, O God!
-port us in the strife, sup-port . . . us in the strife!
strife, sup-port us in the strife, in the strife!
-port . . . . . us in the strife, sup-port us in the strife,
. . . . Sup-port . . . us in the strife, support us in the strife, support us in the
Di-rect us in Thy ways, O God! O God! Support us in the
Di-rect us in Thy
F
O God! O God! support us in the strife, O God! sup-port us in the strife, O
strife, O God! O God! support us in the strife, support us in the strife, O
strife. O God! O God! support us in the strife, sup-port us in the
ways, O God! O God! support us in the strife, sup-port us in the strife, O
fz

God! sup - port us in the strife, O God! sup - port us in the strife, O God!
God! sup - port us in the strife, sup - port us in the strife, sup -
strife! sup - port us in the strife, O God! sup - port us, sup -
God! sup - port us in the strife, sup - port us in the strife, sup -
ff
O God! support, sup - port, sup-port us in the strife! Di-rect us in Thy
- port us, sup - port us, support us in the strife! Di - rect us in Thy
- port us in the strife, support us in the strife!
- port us, support us in the strife, support us in the strife! Di -
Org. Ped.
G
ways, di - rect us in Thy ways, O God! Sup - port us in the strife!
ways, di - rect us in Thy ways, O God! Sup - port us in the strife!
Di-rect us in Thy ways, O God! Sup - port us in the strife!
- rect us in Thy ways, O God! O God! Sup - port us in the strife!
G
fz
fz
Ped.
fz

Printed and bound in Great Britain by
Caligraving Limited Thetford Norfolk

9/96 (25737)